MW01279845

DIVORCE MADE SIMPLE

THE ULTIMATE GUIDE
BY A FORMER FAMILY JUDGE

DIVORCED

LINDA D. SCHOONOVER

Divorce Made Simple
The Ultimate Guide by a Former Family Judge
©2017 Linda D. Schoonover

ISBN 978-0-998-3269-3-1

www.RockyRoadPublishing.com

Dedication

Broken children and families who are too often caught in a court system that refuses to acknowledge them.

THE AUTHOR

Linda Schoonover is a former family judge, attorney, and best selling author. Prior to her election to the circuit court bench in 2010, she was a Board certified family law attorney with her own practice for almost twenty-five years. During that time, she specialized in family law and co-authored the Shared Parental Responsibility portion of the Florida Bar's Family Law Continuing Legal Education Manual. She has more than twenty years experience as a Supreme-court appointed family and civil mediator.

More information about the author, divorce, and mediation is available at LindaSchoonover.com and DivorceMadeSimple.com.

Acknowledgements

Special thanks to my husband, Dave Carley, for his support and to those on my Divorce Made Simple launch team – Nancy Pombo, Cindy McGuire, Jessica McGuire Hage, Marcia Snyder, Candee DeRosier, Jules Fox, Kathryn Townsend, Peri Sedigh, Cindy Lara, Jane Rathbun, Dawn Harris Goodwin, Debbie LeGrand, Beth Hobbs Chiles, Kathleen Beaulieu, Westley Curtiss, Ericka Benfield, Kay Ann Johnson-Waite, Veronika Gasparyan, Jacquelyn Elnor Johnson, Stephen Toroni, Meeghan Moldof, Sally Barker, Ndeye Labadens, Laura Virden Mathis, Carmen S. Miller, Jennifer Englert, Elsa Mendoza, Mitransh Singh Parihar for patiently waiting for the release of this book and the women in the Lady Lawyers Loving Family Law Facebook community-including but not limited to- Jen Benton, Thessica Shauna Harris, Nakeitha Sweeting Hodrick, Germese Gee, Cheryl Fletcher, Jennifer Trabin, Kira Elise, Livia Chaykin, Alyson Lembeck, Adelmis Bohigas Naderpour, Debrakaye Chevian, Ellaretha Coleman, Kyle Kieneck, Christina L. Adkins, Nicole Rofe, Tina Seifert, Kristin Hayes Kirkner, Lisa Knox, Raisa Romaelle, Rosalind Johnson, Marisol Cruz, and Christina Mckinnon and more than two hundred other women attorneys taking it to their practice to the next level.

LEARN MORE AT

DIVORCEMADESIMPLE.COM

TABLE OF CONTENTS

.

INTRODUCTION

As a judge, I once signed a final judgment for a man who waited twenty-six years after he separated from his wife to finalize his divorce.

"Why did you wait so long?" I asked.

The seventy-eight year old man shrugged. "I just couldn't figure out how to get her served."

You may relate to that story if you're going through a divorce and wondering if there is light at the end of the tunnel. Legal issues appear magnified when you combine them with the emotional and financial roller coaster usually experienced in a divorce.

What is stopping you? Are you trying to figure out what step to take next? Are you frustrated by how to pay your household bills at the same time you're dealing with escalating attorney's fees? In either case, this book is for you.

Divorce Made Simple is an easy-to-read guide to help you navigate the legal process and protect you and your children. Courts are ill-equipped to protect those who use the courts as a way to resolve their personal and family issues. Unfortunately, in the process of dissolving your marriage, you may find that you must protect yourself from becoming victims of the system itself. In fact, the longer people remain in the system, the more it threatens their well being and that of their dependents.

Even if you get a fair judge that listens, it is unlikely all the issues will be decided in your favor. Rulings may not appear judicial or fair. Although rulings are supposed to follow the law and prior court decisions, often they do not. Like other professions, judges have different attitudes, demeanors, competence, and experience. Judges may come to the bench with personal or political goals. If you are able to move through the divorce process without losing contact with your children and being destroyed financially, mentally, and emotionally, consider it a win.

A map—not a destination planner. Use this book to map out your divorce, the process, and to determine what principles are generally used by the courts to resolve legal issues. It will arm you with information necessary to have greater control and confidence through every step of the process.

This is your divorce, your children, and your assets. Be wise.

Make this your goal—start with understanding the process the court system uses after a petition is filed. Then, after studying both the short and long term costs of a divorce, you may decide to resolve your divorce as much as possible outside of court. Alternatively, you may seek marriage counseling and remain married or separated.

Practical advice!

This book is not legal advice and should not be used as a substitute for legal advice from an attorney. It is a practical manual about how to get through a divorce from beginning to end with or without an attorney. Even if you have an attorney, this book, may simplify the legal mumbo jumbo and help you avoid pitfalls that could wipe out monies you had originally earmarked for retirement or your children's college education.

How to use this book

To keep it simple, the book has three primary sections—Path, Process, and Principles.

The *Path section* includes a review of divorce alternatives and issues to consider before filing.

In the *Process section,* you will learn what and how to file a petition for divorce and issues to consider when and before filing, what to look for when choosing an attorney, how to handle discovery issues, and an overview of the mediation and collaborative processes.

The *Principles section* is an overview of some of the principles used by courts to resolve issues of parental and residential responsibility, equitable distribution, alimony, child support, and attorney's fees. After reading this section, you should have a better understanding of legal terms, factors, and analyses most commonly used by the courts.

Disclaimer

This is not intended as legal advice and you are not my client. This book is for informational purposes only. You should rely only on the advice of an attorney who is aware of the specific facts of your case and the law in the state in which you reside. Be aware that divorce laws differ somewhat in every state.

Legal Warning

The content of this book is provided with the understanding that the Publisher and Author are not providing legal, financial, therapeutic, or other professional advice. Some of the content may not apply to your unique circumstances. For advice regarding your particular situation, you must seek counsel from the appropriate professional.

Opinions, views, and statements expressed by the publisher and author are theirs alone.

THE PATH

CHAPTER 1

BEFORE FILING FOR
DIVORCE CONSIDER...

Why are you seeking a divorce?

Divorce is a major life event.

Understanding why you're ending your marriage may be even more important than your initial decision to marry. Obviously, you can always rationalize or justify a divorce, but beyond feeling justified, angry, or hurt, why do you believe your marriage is over?

The path to getting your final judgment may feel like a long, dark tunnel to a pit that is hard to escape. Many endure an emotional roller coaster, high attorney's fees, and fallout from the court system itself, with lasting consequences that can't always be predicted or undone. If I had a ten dollar bill for every person who got divorced, and after one or more years changed their minds and regretted it— well, you know—I'd be rich. From my experience, the reason a marriage falls apart is not because of the actions or attitude of one spouse. In most cases, both parties are responsible for the decline in the relationship.

Before moving ahead, consider the short term and long term consequences of a divorce. Your children's lives will be shaped during and after, by you and your spouse's behavior and the process itself. Like you, they will also experience their own emotional roller coaster and if it is a long and high conflict divorce, they may become traumatized and their health may even be permanently impacted.

A protracted divorce could threaten your financial security. Judges may order your assets used for payment of attorney fees, expert fees, and even psychological evaluations. You may have little control over the court's decision as to what asset to liquidate, when, or for what purpose. Savings accounts, retirement accounts, whole life insurance policies, and even your home may ultimately be liquidated for attorney fees before your divorce is finalized. Unfortunately, these types of orders are common and are not always within the court's authority. However, appealing such decisions may do little than incur additional attorney fees.

Finally, your relationship with your spouse will be, if not completely destroyed, at least, significantly altered. It is easier to pull the trigger on a divorce than to work towards reconciliation. Normally once a petition is filed, an invisible line is drawn in the sand. Because of pride, embarrassment, or anger, one or both spouses may believe that it is too late to back out and seek reconciliation. A trust has been broken that may never be renewed.

Before any major life change, it is wise to seek counseling. Are you reacting from anger or an emotion that changes from day to day? Or is your decision well thought out, reasonable, and rational?

Advice from an objective mental health professional may encourage you to rethink your decision. It could also reframe or reinforce your commitment to proceed. If you do not have a counselor, make your own list of the pros and cons and write your reasons for seeking a divorce. Deciding to divorce before understanding the "why" charts a course with very few places for a u-turn.

Coming up...

Alternatives to divorce that may give you a temporary, if not the permanent resolution to your marital issues.

NOTES

CHAPTER 2

WHAT IS YOUR ALTERNATIVE?

It is usually "the last straw" that sends a party running to divorce court. When that happens, impulse and emotion often overcome common sense and rational thinking. Although divorce alternatives may not relieve all the pressure points in your marriage, it may make sense to review your options.

What if you just move out for a while?
The Pros and Cons of a physical separation.

Physically living apart may give one or both of you time to decide independently if a divorce is what you need or want.

Some states require a physical separation for a certain amount of time before a divorce. Technically this may be called "separated from bed or board" in your petition for dissolution. It means you have not had sex with your spouse for certain period of time. Although you may have to abide by a statutory time frame which is the time from filing your divorce petition to the granting of the divorce final judgment, sexual intimacy with your spouse is generally outside the court's interest.

Caution!

Throughout your separation and divorce, make sure that your actions do not communicate the wrong impression to the court. For example, the court may see your decision to leave the marital home as a disinterest in retaining the home. Similarly telling the court that you are afraid to leave your children with your spouse because of their lack of parenting skills or some addictive behavior may be unbelievable if you regularly leave your children with your spouse.

What if you're being abused?

If you have been a victim of spouse abuse, you may file an emergency petition for protection against domestic violence, which, if granted, will immediately provide a legal and enforceable separation from your spouse. It may not guarantee your continued exclusive possession of the home or financial support. All jurisdictions are different and judges may have limitations that prevent them from offering the relief that you are seeking. Alternatively, seek a safe house if you or your children are victims of domestic violence and you do not have sufficient monies to move to a different residence.

The filing of an injunction should only be used when there has been or there is a genuine fear of domestic violence in the immediate future. Do not use a petition for protection to gain an advantage in court. The filing and service of a petition for an injunction will immediately sever all contact between you and your spouse. If a judge finds that the allegations within the petition are false or fraudulent, that may affect their decision regarding your timesharing with the minor children and the judge's opinion of your credibility.

Caution! Your failure to attend the injunction hearing (if scheduled) may result in your petition being dismissed and your spouse being abled to have continued and ongoing contact with you.

Can you file for Legal Separation?

Some states allow you to file for a legal separation. In this proceeding, the court determines the rights and responsibilities of both people during a specific period. The petition may be similar to a dissolution petition, however, it will not request a termination of the marriage. Some states require a list of reasons why a legal separation is necessary. Others only require the typical no-fault allegations such as the parties desire to live apart. A legal separation only determines the temporary rights and responsibilities of the parties and does not prohibit either person from seeking a dissolution of marriage at that time or later.

Receiving financial support without filing for divorce. What is a petition for separate maintenance

Although some states, such as Florida, do not recognize a legal separation, they will allow you to file a petition for separate maintenance. This temporary order addresses issues such as child support, visitation, and alimony. A separate maintenance action begins like a dissolution of marriage with the filing of a petition.

Can your marriage be annulled?

An annulment, like a divorce, is a final order, but it is based on the circumstances at the time of the marriage. For example, the petition may claim that one person consented to the marriage under fraud, was underage, or was under the influence of drugs or alcohol when the marriage took place. A spouse being married to another person at the time of the marriage or the parties not consummating the marriage may be other reasons for an annulment.

Coming up …

If alternate remedies or temporary separations are infeasible, your next step is deciding if your marriage is irretrievably broken. In the next chapter, we will review what to do to allege that your marriage is irretrievably broken.

NOTES

CHAPTER 3

IS YOUR MARRIAGE IRRETRIEVABLY BROKEN?

During a final hearing when a couple approached me for entry of their final judgment, I'd ask why they thought their marriage was irretrievably broken. I watched couples stop and look at each other. It was clear that one of them had become so engrossed in the process and the adversarial proceedings, they'd forgotten why they filed for a divorce.

Irretrievably broken means there is no way to reconcile and fix your marriage. Although many states no longer require the judges to ask the question, some states still require it. Think about this before your final hearing and preferably before you file a petition or retain an attorney.

What is "no fault?"

Before no-fault divorce, people had to prove that their spouse was at fault in some way. Now, most states have a no-fault divorce law. Most of you will no longer have to prove how the other person "wronged" you—just saying you want a divorce along with the words that your marriage is "irretrievably broken" is enough.

Coming up…

In the next chapter, we will review the steps you need to take if you know a divorce is what you need or want.

NOTES

CHAPTER 4

WHAT TO DO AFTER YOU DECIDE TO DIVORCE

Divorce laws vary from state to state. In every state, however, divorce, or dissolution of marriage, as it is sometimes called, is a judicial process that terminates a marriage and restores a person to the status of single. It is usually finalized by a judge, a hearing officer, or a general magistrate. In addition to the goal of ending a marriage, divorce proceedings also include decisions relating to spousal support (generally referred to as alimony), child support, child custody (also known as residential responsibility) and property and debt distribution (generally known as equitable distribution or community property) as well as issues concerning payment of attorney's fees, and life and health insurance.

Understand the short and long term consequences

Prior to taking any action to legally end your marriage, consult a family law attorney to assure that you understand the short and long-term legal consequences. Then, assuming there is no fear of domestic violence, speak to your spouse about your decision. Express your desire to make the process as amicable as possible and inquire as to their possible willingness to attend mediation to work out the terms of an uncontested divorce.

What is the difference between a contested and uncontested divorce?

If both spouses agree to the terms before or after filing for the divorce, it is referred to as an *uncontested divorce*. If there are one or more unresolved issues such as alimony, child support, child custody, or equitable distribution, it is referred to as a *contested divorce*.

Uncontested divorces are usually less expensive and resolved faster. Often a divorce begins as contested, but after mediation or another alternative resolution process, it becomes uncontested. Mediation can be scheduled before either person files any paperwork with the court or before you retain an attorney. Read more about how to prepare for mediation in a later chapter.

Give your spouse time to consider your decision before moving ahead.

Prior to scheduling a mediation, give your spouse ample time to consider your decision. Divorce evokes deep feelings of loss and grief and it is important to allow your spouse time to process these feelings. A divorce is an emotional roller coaster and although giving your spouse time may initially delay the start of the divorce, it may clear out some of the emotional obstacles that escalate attorney's fees and create greater delays. From my experience, no one handles a divorce or loss the same way and the time required to work through these emotions also differs. For these reasons alone, it is beneficial for each party to find their own licensed mental health counselor to help them during the pendency of the divorce.

Can you use a simplified divorce process?

Some states have a simplified process that you may use if you have no disputed issues, no children, and no property for the court to divide. This process will reduce the time and money usually spent by others with more complex issues.

Action point!

Call the clerk of court in the area where you or your spouse live and ask if there is a simplified divorce process. If so, one or both of you will need to go to the courthouse and sign a joint petition. If you have a completed a final judgment of dissolution of marriage, ask when the judge sets hearings to enter final judgments.

What if you have a prenuptial agreement?

If you and your spouse signed a prenuptial prior to your marriage, then the steps for receiving a final judgment may be as simple as attaching the agreement to a simplified petition and the proposed final judgment and asking the court to accept and ratify the agreement. So long as there is no disagreement about the terms in the agreement, the circumstances under which it was signed or under which the agreement is enforceable, your divorce may be fast and simple. Step one – find the agreement and review the terms. Step two, give a copy (you want to safeguard the original) to your spouse to make sure there are no issues that would keep you from proceeding.

What are forms of legal assistance can you use other than a private attorney?

Paralegal services. You may have seen an ad for a "divorce" for $199, $299, or $399. Document preparers are a form of legal service providers that should carry a buyer beware sticker. Preparers are generally not attorneys, may not be paralegals, and may have no legal experience at all. For example, inadvertently checking "sole custody" as opposed to "shared parental responsibility", or stating the terms of child support or visitation incorrectly could create unintended consequences. Other critical issues such as the transfer of real property and duration of alimony, when stated incorrectly, could also result in serious financial risks. If you are not divorce savvy and do not understand legal terminology, you may sign and agree to terms unintentionally or inadvertently. (See, for example, the Parenting Responsibility chapter in this book). If that happens, unless your spouse agrees to a modification, you risk incurring exorbitant legal fees after entry of the final judgment to correct the mistake.

Pro se coordinators. With the influx of self-represented litigants (who are generally referred to courts as pro se litigants), some counties now offer *pro se coordinators* who offer forms and assistance. Since this department is typically within the courthouse and usually operated by someone associated with a family court judge or a family division, they may be able to provide pleading forms and instructions for assuring that you take the right steps within their jurisdiction to receive your final judgment.

Legal Aid. If you are below a certain income level, you may qualify for a *legal aid attorney.* Legal aid offices are generally nonprofit organizations partially funded through government grants. Some offices use their own paid attorneys who provide services to clients in limited areas of practice such as divorce. They also may use private attorneys willing to provide pro bono (free) services to individuals who qualify.

Hot tip!

From my experience and observation, most judges prefer to work with attorneys rather than to deal with unrepresented litigants. If you pursue your divorce without counsel, you may perceive that judges are biased against you. However, to ensure fairness to both sides, they will normally not allow you to break evidentiary or court rules because you are unrepresented.

Second, judges become familiar, often in professional, if not personal circles with attorneys they regularly see in their courtroom.

While they should not refer to attorneys by their first name, occasionally it happens. Although you may perceive this means that this relationship will prevent you from receiving a fair trial, it does not always mean that. However, hiring an attorney who regularly practices in front of the judge may eliminate this possibility and give you a slight advantage because of their knowledge of the judge's certain idiosyncrasies and preferences.

Coming up...

If you have determined that your divorce will require the professional advice of an attorney, choosing the right attorney is not as easy as looking at ads or talking to your friends. The next chapter uncovers some of the minefields that could destroy your chances of a reasonable divorce or a successful attorney-client relationship.

NOTES

CHAPTER 5

HOW TO CHOOSE AN ATTORNEY

Choosing an attorney is difficult. Do you pick the one with the most ads, the best ads, or the one that your friend used?

Do they have the three c's?

Rather than reading ads and only asking your friends about the attorney who helped them "win" their case, interview attorneys and look for those with these three c's—competent, caring, and cost conscious.

Although it may create an initial delay in the filing of your petition and even the payment of multiple consultation fees, if possible, consult with three different lawyers. What you learn about the process and how different attorneys practice may save you thousands of dollars and a much greater delay if you have to switch attorneys later.

Does the attorney's skill and experience match your need?

A consultation should clarify your divorce options and issues. Does the attorney help you understand ways to resolve your case or are they encouraging immediate litigation? Are they also a mediator? Do they feel as comfortable in the courtroom as they do in mediation? Listen, make notes, and ask questions.

Caution!

If the attorney advises you before you have provided your background information, beware. Not knowing your unique facts and what you are seeking in the divorce may indicate a lack of experience and sensitivity to nuances in divorce matters. It may, on the other hand, just indicate you have found someone with a big ego. In either case, consider consulting another attorney.

As you listen to the attorney's spiel about themselves or their practice, think about how your needs match their abilities and experience. Do they have the experience to handle your divorce?

Competent/Trustworthy

Whenever you hire any professional, make sure you choose one you think you can trust and the one with the level of experience and expertise that you need to present your case. An uncontested matter will generally require less experience and expertise than a contested matter.

Not all attorneys are experts in divorce but not all divorces require an expert. Your attorney's knowledge and experience should when possible, match the level of experience and expertise necessary to complete your matter. However, because some advertise that they practice divorce, but rarely do and others have years of experience but don't advertise themselves as experts, to determine an attorney's experience will generally require that you personally meet and consult with them.

Recent law school graduates may know the law enough to pass the bar exam, but may not have the necessary experience to handle a complex divorce. Law school does not teach anyone how to practice. That only comes with experience.

How important are credentials?

Don't let credentials be the only way you qualify an attorney. First, consider the attorney's communication skills. Are they personable and easy to talk to or gruff and arrogant? A gruff, arrogant attorney may be a strong advocate in court or have extensive experience, but if you want an amicable resolution, someone with strong emotional intelligence may be a better choice than even someone who is a bulldog in court.

Many states have certification programs for attorneys to set themselves apart from others based upon their expertise. Very few attorneys are board certified and they generally come with a higher price tag. A board certified attorney may have initially passed an exam, like a bar exam, in marital and family law and are also required to keep up with changes in family law. However, being board certified doesn't guarantee they are ethical, smarter, or a better communicator. Nor does it suggest they are caring or cost conscious. If a lawyer has years of experience and is caring and cost conscious, choosing one who is "board certified" may not be the best choice.

Questions to ask during your consultation

Do they seem to genuinely care about you and your case? If you are bothered by their "bedside manner" or lack thereof, they may have a reputation in the legal community for being difficult. This is why your observations about the office and staff paired with questions about an attorney's background are crucial.

If the attorney asks for an amount of money in advance to secure his services (retainer) and the amount seems inflated or the attorney instills fear about your case and how much expertise it will take to resolve it—stop, go home and give yourself time to think about their comments. If the attorney bases the retainer on the cost of a trial, and their strategy is "always to go to trial," it may be time for you to do more research about them as well as your ability and willingness to commit to a trial before you have even filed a petition. Most cases settle and it is only the most adversarial that go to trial. The adversarial posture of a case may be the result of the unwillingness of the parties or the attorneys to settle.

If cases go to trial, the divorce is set to last longer than six months and to require multiple hearings and consume much more attorney time than those that settle after mediation. If you have assets including businesses valued at millions of dollars and believe that your divorce will require experts and multiple days of trial, a retainer of twenty five or fifty thousand dollars may be justified, but retainers are generally nonrefundable. (See next chapter for more information about retainers and attorney fees.) After paying a high retainer and then having your case resolve two days or even a month later during a mediation, may mean you have paid too much or the estimated time and skill to finish your divorce was overinflated.

Will you be a good client?

Attorneys have their own purpose for a consultation. In addition to acquiring a new client and new monies to continue their practice, they need to uncover and understand the legal and factual issues in your case. They may also need to determine if you are a good fit for their practice and if this is a case they want to accept. In order to do that, the attorney will ask personal information about you, your spouse, your marriage and why you are seeking a divorce. This information is necessary to advise you about what to expect from them or the courts regarding your divorce. Their advice may be skewed if you fail to give the attorney an accurate or complete information.

Check off these questions during your consultation

1. Does the attorney seem interested in the facts of your case?

Do they ask what you want as an outcome or simply tell you what and how much to go after in your divorce? Remember, this person will be sending you a bill every month. If you don't get along after one hour or there is something that does not seem right, look for a different attorney.

2. Do they use the consult time only to explain what they expect from you and why you should hire them?

3. Are you introduced to their staff? What is your comfort level with them? How much experience do they have? How frustrated will you be if you speak to a paralegal or legal assistant more often than the attorney?

4. How are tasks and responsibilities divided between the attorney and their staff?

5. How long has the attorney practiced family law and how often are they in court?

    Ask how many trials they have had, not how many they have "won." Remember—no one really wins in a divorce. You might have some success in the court's rulings, but the court has great latitude in family matters.

6. Observe the office. Does it seem to run smoothly? Is it cluttered or tidy? This could indicate a recent trial or an unorganized office.

7. Was the front office person pleasant? Often the receptionist is the only employee a sole practitioner will have after beginning their practice. How often will you speak to that individual as your law office liaison?

8. Is the attorney board certified? Do they specialize in marital and family law? Retaining a board-certified attorney usually means that your retainer will be two or three times what the

retainer will be for someone just starting out and may also mean hourly rates with the same multiplication factor.

9. Is the attorney a new law school graduate or did they graduate fifty years ago?

10. Is the firm computerized? Paperless? Do they use snail mail or Have they advanced to email and texts? What are the billing practices? Do they bill monthly? Do they itemize and record the time each task takes?

11. Do they offer ways to keep your bill manageable? Will they make decisions without your input because you hired them "to take care of the divorce" for you?

12. How do they prepare for hearings? If possible, go to court and watch them and others. How prepared do they appear? Do they appear to have a working relationship with the judge?

13. Do they have personal or professional relationships with psychologists?

14. Do they lay out a plan for your divorce that includes delay, deceit or disparagement of your spouse? Ask them, and then ask yourself if this is the path you want to take.

15. Do they tell you you're going to trial because they always go to trial?

16. What does your gut tell you? Are you prepared to trust this person with advice that affects the rest of your life?

17. What's the average cost for a divorce?

18. How often should you expect to hear from them about the status of your divorce?

19. How will they communicate with you? Text, email, telephone or by letter?

20. How would you reach them if you had a question? How would you reach them if there was an emergency?

21. Do they let you know about their conversations with opposing counsel and the court? If so, when would you become aware of these communications?

22. How many cases do they typically handle at one time?

23. What's the average time it takes to complete a divorce in this office?

24. Does the attorney recommend that you stop talking to your spouse? If so, why? If there are domestic violence issues and escalating conflict, then restricting communication may be wise. If not, this may hinder getting a less expensive, amicable divorce. If your communication with your spouse always goes through the attorney, expect delays, higher fees and increased personal frustration and anger.

25. Does the attorney guarantee that you will win? Do they say they are "in" with all the judges and can make it happen? This may reveal not only his character, but may alert you to judicial politics within the county or district. If you hear this, it might be in your interest to consult with a different attorney or resolve your issues outside of court.

26. Does the attorney have a history of ethical sanctions? There are more grievances filed in family law than any other. Although this does not always reflect the level of service or expertise of the attorney, if the attorney has received ethical sanctions by the state bar, ask what they have done to alleviate similar complaints.

27. Does the attorney practice in the county in which you will serve the petition. Usually, this is the county in which you or your spouse live.

Don't make these assumptions!

1. Don't assume the attorney can or will be willing to work with you on a payment plan. A law firm is a business. Unless there is a sign on the door that says "Legal Aid," it is not. With the number of attorneys glutting the market, it is harder and harder for attorneys to remain in business.

2. Don't assume legal services are or should be free. This is especially true if you are friends or family. Giving away their knowledge expertise does not provide an avenue for attorneys to pay their staff.

3. Don't assume they will automatically represent you. Sometimes attorneys will decide not to represent you because of the complexity of the divorce, the attorney on the other side, or their perception that you may be a difficult client.

4. Don't assume it's pay as you go. Your attorney is not a bank. Expect to pay a retainer and a consultation fee. Most people use a major credit card to pay for a retainer. Retainers normally vary depending on the complexity of the divorce but assume that you will pay at least a $2,500 retainer.

5. Don't assume attorneys are perfect because they have a law degree. Just like any other professional, you may run into attorneys with character and behavior issues. Although hopefully few and far between, you may find a few who drink at work. Some may use drugs. Some may lack work ethic and do as little work for as much money as possible. Some may even try to hit on you. They may ask you to lie in court. They may not remember court dates or communicate hearing dates to you. Trust your gut when consulting with an attorney. If it doesn't feel right, leave.

6. Don't assume the attorney will review a box of pleadings or

documents during your consultation and give you an opinion while you wait curbside. This is not a fast food chain, nor is it the purpose of the consultation. In fact, if you appear over demanding, the attorney may raise the retainer or decline to represent you.

7. Don't assume that communication with you will be a top priority regardless of the amount of your retainer. If you want frequent communication and status reports, set up a system for accomplishing this before you write a check. Don't rely on the attorney to have a system in place.

8. Don't assume the attorney will refund your retainer if you change your mind about them or the divorce. Most of the retainers are non-refundable and go immediately into the attorney's practice account.

Frequently Asked Questions

1. **Will the attorney I talk with in a consultation file an answer for me if I don't retain him?**

   Unless and until they have been officially retained, and you have signed a retainer agreement, attorneys usually will not agree to file any pleadings on your behalf.

2. **Can the attorney represent me and my spouse if it is an uncontested divorce?**

   Normally, representing both spouses at the same time creates a conflict of interest. Some states have ethical rules which prevent it. It can also create a malpractice risk for the attorney. An alternative would be to attend mediation with a mediator who will explain and speak to both of you about the divorce process and mediation but will not be able to give legal advice to either of you that might strengthen your position over that of your spouse's.

3. **Will the information I share with my attorney be confidential?**

Yes, the information shared by and with your attorney remains confidential because of the attorney-client privilege.

4. **Will the attorney I talk with during a consultation represent my spouse if he consults with him/her too?**

After a consultation, an attorney may be prohibited from representing your spouse because of confidential information they have received from you, which might assist your spouse and prejudice you. If you file for divorce and the attorney with whom you consulted and shared confidential information represents your spouse, file a motion and ask that the attorney be removed because of a conflict of interest.

5. **Is it okay to bring my friend to the consultation with me?**

You may bring a friend with the warning that their presence may waive your privilege of confidentiality since the privilege only belongs to you and the attorney. In other words, your friend could technically be asked to repeat what you or your attorney discussed in the consultation despite your attorney-client privilege.

6. **Can I tape record the consultation?**

Although that depends on the attorney, make sure that you seek permission of anyone before you tape record them.

Coming up…

Obviously, your decision about which attorney to retain may depend in part on the amount of legal retainer or how successful you are in negotiating a lower amount. In the next chapter, we'll look at how to save money and avoid traps that can cost you thousands of dollars if you decide to hire an attorney.

NOTES

CHAPTER 6

UNDERSTANDING
YOUR LEGAL FEES

An attorney may quote you a retainer of anywhere between two thousand and a hundred thousand dollars. No, that isn't a mistake. Unfortunately, attorney fees in a divorce can run even more than that. Not many people have that much to spend or even the means to acquire that much money for a divorce, let alone a retainer. Even if you don't pay this amount as a retainer when you initially hire an attorney, if your divorce is hotly contested and prolonged over a period of six months or less, your fees could swell to more than a hundred thousand dollars. Before you retain an attorney, there are some things you need to know about your agreement with an attorney.

What is a retainer?

Most attorneys require that you sign a retainer agreement with them before they initiate any legal work. The retainer is a payment in advance for work that an attorney anticipates having to do in your matter.

The retainer agreement should indicate that the money paid as a retainer is refundable or nonrefundable. If it is nonrefundable, that means that regardless of the amount of work completed, that money has been deemed earned. The attorney may justify this as the work that they had to forego or turn away because of your case.

If possible, try to negotiate the retainer amount or the terms of the retainer, so that if you change your mind about the attorney or proceeding with the divorce, some of this money is refundable to you or can be used for other legal services.

The retainer should also outline how and for what services you will be billed.

Are there lower retainers for uncontested divorces?

Most individuals with contested issues will want an attorney to help them in some capacity. Although there may be some contested issues, many attorneys will assist clients at a lower cost as long as they agree that the divorce is "uncontested", that the attorneys will not be required to attend court hearings and clients use only alternate resolution methods such as mediation or collaborative divorce. Attorneys may also agree to represent clients for a limited purpose, such as attending a temporary hearing, mediation, or a domestic violence hearing.

Know the answers to these questions before signing a retainer agreement

1. Will you be billed for telephone calls, texts, and emails?

2. Are you automatically billed for two-tenths or three-tenths of an hour for texts and emails? Are you billed for the secretary's time? For legal assistants time? Are there items for which the attorney does not charge?

3. Are there different amounts charged for court time, travel time or office time? Will you be double billed when two attorneys are speaking about your case in the office or when the attorney gives instructions to the paralegal about your case?

4. Will the attorney automatically charge your credit card when the retainer has been used? If you do not pay your bill timely, does the attorney have your consent to automatically withdraw from your case?

Can you get your file back if you don't pay your bill?

Often state laws allow attorneys to have a retaining lien on your file. This may or may not be explained by the attorney or within your fee agreement. A retaining lien allows the office to retain the file. If you want to change attorneys, you may believe that you will be able to pick up your file. However, the file, whether electronic or physical, is the office file and belongs to the attorney and is not a file that you own. The attorney's office will generally copy the file for you, without the attorney's personal notes once you have paid any outstanding bill.

What if you have a problem with your attorney?

If you have problems with your attorney or their office staff, schedule a time when you can speak one-on-one with the attorney. If you are not receiving copies of the pleadings from the office or are not being notified in advance of hearings and other developments in your case, a short conversation may be all that's necessary to rectify the problem. However, if it's an issue that may significantly impact the outcome of your case and can't be resolved to your satisfaction, it may be better to leave, find a different attorney, and give up any unused retainer (negotiating the amount, in the beginning, could save you money here).

There are avenues for negotiation once you have left the practice, such as contacting the state bar association's consumer line for options and ideas regarding the resolution of the dispute.

Caution: Changing attorneys often may make it increasingly more difficult to retain an attorney or to retain them for a reasonable retainer amount. Clients may develop a reputation within the legal community or within the court system itself for being difficult or flaky. Knowing that a potential client has had three or four prior attorneys usually signals to the new attorney, that there are potential problems with a case or with the client.

Five tips to reduce your attorney's fees from the start

1. **Telephone time**. Every time you call the attorney's office and speak to the attorney, legal assistant, or paralegal, you may be charged. (Refer to your retainer agreement). Save your questions until you can ask at least three, so a minimum charge isn't billed for each call. You may also just save your questions until you meet with the attorney. Alternatively, you can ask to speak to the legal assistant who may not charge you or charge less than the attorney or paralegal.

2. **Handholding**. Being upset is normal when you are going through a divorce. You may be afraid, angry, and feel a host of other emotions. However, most of these feelings have to do with the disruption of your expectations and future unknowns. A psychologist or counselor can help address these fears— an attorney can't. Find a good counselor before you file for a divorce or as soon as you can after you've been served. The counselor can suggest ways to deal with your fears, communicate with your spouse during the pending divorce as well as how to tell your children about your decision to divorce.

3. **Unnecessary discovery.** If emotions are driving your divorce, your legal fees will escalate. If you're desperate to find out every cent your spouse is hiding, every cent they have spent on the other person, and want the judge to tear them apart for their bad actions, you're asking for a financially disastrous divorce. Typically, the more you spend, the less satisfied you will be with

your attorney's representation and the end result. If you find yourself anxious or depressed, find a counselor immediately or schedule an appointment with your doctor. Purposefully look for ways to fill your life with positive activities and people.

4. **Avoid having the attorney gather and organize financial documents**. If your attorney or his staff has to continue to call you to set up times for you to come in with the discovery and then organize it for you, that adds up to more attorney fees. If you can't do the task yourself, ask a family member, friend or a bookkeeper to assist you. Paying a third person or thanking them with a dinner or other gift will cost less than what an attorney may have to charge you for the same thing. In addition, ask the attorney in advance for a list of documents that are required by the state's compliance statute and gather and organize the documents.

5. **Limit depositions** Limiting the number of the depositions will reduce attorney fees as well as the court reporter time and transcription costs. Shortening the length of your depositions and narrowing the subject matter will also pay off. Scheduling depositions just to retaliate or embarrass a person generally results only in more attorney fees and costs, but little that you can use in future hearings or trials. If you have an attorney, you are paying for their preparation of questions and attendance at the depositions. If you must depose witnesses, create a list of questions and give the list to the attorney in advance of the deposition.

Frequently Asked Questions:

Can I get my retainer back if I change my mind and want a different attorney to represent me?

Retainers can be refundable or nonrefundable. If they are refundable, you will be able to receive the monies less any costs and fees already billed by the attorney. If you haven't signed a retainer, ask if the monies are refundable or nonrefundable. If you have already signed a retainer agreement, reread the contract.

Will I be billed when I call and ask the attorney questions?

Certainly, you can call the attorney's office, but actually talking with the attorney to ask questions may be different. For busy law offices, questions are usually funneled through legal assistants. Frequently calling the office and demanding that you speak with the lawyer could leave you with a hefty price tag that you can't pay and earn the reputation within the office as a pest. If you need to speak to the attorney, wait until you have at least three questions and then schedule for a specific time.

If my attorney and the legal assistant are in the same room during a session, will I be billed for their time?

Typically, that depends on the attorneys practice and should be addressed before you sign a retainer agreement.

Coming up...

Now that you have determined if your case is uncontested or contested, chosen an attorney or have decided to go solo, it is time to begin understanding the basic building blocks of a divorce (pleadings) and the process that you will use to file them. In the next chapter, we will begin with an understanding of the first pleading in a divorce, the petition, and the allegations that must be filed within that pleading.

THE PROCESS

CHAPTER 7

DRAFT, SIGN, AND FILE

Before filing anything, you need to become familiar with pleadings including a petition for divorce, an answer, and other documents that are served with a petition. The beginning phase of a divorce is usually marked with the filing of a petition for divorce and the service of the petition on your spouse.

Representing yourself in a divorce is like learning any other new area— it is a bit overwhelming until you invest the time. If you have an attorney, this chapter should help you make sense of the pleadings you review and approve.

What is a petition for divorce?

A petition is the first pleading filed in the divorce process. The petition must include statutory allegations, such as names and residences of the parties, that the marriage is irretrievably broken, and that you have lived in the state for the time period required by statute. If you have minor children or property, the petition will allege the names and birthdates of the minor children, the location of marital properties, and a statement asking for specific relief.

Customarily, the petition is signed by you or your attorney and includes the name of the court with jurisdiction over the matter, such as a circuit court, and is typically titled, "Petition for Divorce" or

"Petition for Dissolution of Marriage."

Where can you find a form?

If you are not represented by counsel, a form for a petition for dissolution or a petition for divorce may be found by going to your state supreme court's website and downloading a document by that name, checking with your local law library, or seeking the assistance of an attorney, legal clinic, or mediator. The Appendix contains links to the resources each state provides for litigants. Some are more 'pro se' friendly than others.

Key details to get right before drafting your petition

Whether you are handling the divorce yourself as a pro se litigant (one unrepresented by counsel) or are working with an attorney, failing to meet the residency requirements or filing in the wrong place or court could ultimately scrub the launch of your petition.

How long have you lived in the state?

Check your state statute regarding the length of time required to reside in the state before you file for divorce. This requirement may vary from thirty days to six months. The Appendix at the back of the book provides the residency requirement for each state.

Are you filing in the right court?

Does the court have the authority to make decisions in your case? The state legislature or constitution typically mandates what types of cases a court can hear. For example, Florida circuit court judges preside over divorce cases. (However, what level of judges handle divorce matters and how they are titled may vary from state to state).

Action step!

Call the clerk of court in the area in which you or your spouse lives and ask the name of court with jurisdiction to hear your case.

What should you ask for?

The petition sets forth the issues and puts your spouse and the court on notice as to what relief you are seeking. If and when applicable, your petition should specifically request alimony, child support, visitation, or time sharing with your children, a division of the debts and assets and, when necessary, reasonable attorney's fees.

If you do not have children or real property and are not seeking support, your request may be simply that you want a divorce. Some states refer to this as a "simplified divorce".

If there are minor children, you will need to ask the court to determine that it is in the children's best interest that you and your spouse have shared parental responsibility. If you want the children to live with you or spend time split between you and your spouse, you may need to ask for primary residential responsibility, joint parental responsibility, or sole parental responsibility. For an explanation of terms, refer to the Principles section in this book.

You may request a court to equitably divide the marital property or debts. The court may divide property accumulated during the marriage (marital) or specifically order a transfer of certain property to you and other property to your spouse. For example, you may request that the marital home be granted to you or that it be sold. Property subject to division may include real estate, tangible, intangible and personal assets.

If you're in need of alimony or spousal support, whether temporary or permanent, you will need to allege your need and your spouse's ability to pay. For more general information about the legal terms used when drafting allegations about issues of residential responsibility, child support, equitable distribution, and alimony, refer to the Principles section of this book.

What if you have a prenuptial?

If you previously entered into a premarital, a prenuptial, or post-marital agreement, it must be attached to the petition with a statement, if true, that all issues have been resolved and the parties are prepared to enter a final judgment based upon the agreement.

Preparing a Petition—The basics

The first page of the petition will include the name of the court in which the petition is filed – such as *Seventh Judicial Circuit.* You will need to include a place at the top of the page for the Clerk to insert a Case number. For example *"Case Number-_____.*

At the top of the first page to the left will be what attorneys call the style of the case. The style of the case generally includes the type of matter (in a divorce it might be labeled – *In re: The Marriage*) and the names of the parties. For example if Betty White and Robert White were to file for a divorce the style would be:

In re the marriage of (the type of legal matter)
Betty White, Petitioner, (the person who filed)
and Robert White, Respondent (person who will respond-
the spouse)

Following the court reference at the top, the case number, and the name of the parties, the title of the pleading is centered. It will read *Petition for Dissolution of Marriage or Petition for Divorce.*

Typical allegations within a petition might be as follows:

Type of action. This is an action for dissolution of marriage between _____ and _____.

Jurisdiction. _____ has been a resident of the state of _____ for more than _____ months prior to filing the petition.

The marriage of the parties. The parties were married in _____ in (year).

Irretrievably broken. The marriage is irretrievably broken.

Minor children.

The parties have two children ages six and ten. The Petitioner requests that the parties have shared parental responsibility and it is in the best interests of the minor children that the Petitioner have primary residential responsibility.

Marital home.

The parties have a marital home titled in both names; however, the Petitioner requests exclusive possession of the marital home; both temporarily and post judgment.

Relief

Wherefore, the wife seeks judgment dissolving the marriage, the residential responsibility of the minor children, an award of the marital home, and an equal distribution of other marital properties.

    Signature
    Printed name
    Address
    Telephone number
    Email address

Where and what to file?

Your petition and the pleadings accompanying the petition are filed with the clerk of the court. The clerk is a record keeper for the court. If you file a petition with the clerk, do not assume the judge receives a copy. Except for emergency hearings, when clerks usually provide a copy of the pleadings and file to the judge, judges do not receive and are not aware of any pleading filed in a matter until they request the file for a hearing.

What other documents are served with a petition?

The clerk will issue a summons when you file the petition. The summons provides information to your spouse regarding their need to respond to the petition within a certain time and manner and begins the stop watch for their response.

Action step!

Complete a financial affidavit before you file a petition for dissolution. It will help you determine your financial needs, assess your income and liabilities, and provide you with an outline for creating a list of your assets and their value. It is a prerequisite for receiving alimony or child support and is usually filed with your divorce petition.

How to prepare a financial affidavit

Financial affidavits are available in different forms depending on the income of the party or the type of action that is pending. For example, the affidavit may be brief for purposes of child support enforcement or, if the other party's annual income is above a certain statutory amount, it may be a long form. Long forms are especially important in cases where additional details are required.. Although the most time consuming to prepare, it is the most thorough and will detailing your need for alimony or child support by documenting your expenses or income. For example in cases where there are minor children with special needs, it may justify a departure from customary child support guidelines.

Hot tip!

One of the most important documents in a divorce is the financial affidavit. Judges rely on the accuracy of the document to determine child support, alimony, and the distribution of assets and liabilities.

Do not guess when filling out your financial affidavit. Be prepared to justify every number. Guessing usually results in rounding off numbers to the nearest hundred.

Attorneys and judges who have reviewed hundreds of financial affidavits will immediately notice when a party has estimated the expenses on an affidavit. A rounded off number for each category, for example, $100 on clothes, $200 for electricity, and $800 for food, would flag the attorney and judge that you have guessed as to the amounts. If you guess high, it may be that you are padding the numbers for your own benefit. Inaccurate amounts may not only affect your credibility with the judge but may make a difference in the financial relief you receive.

How should you respond to a petition for divorce?

An answer is a response to a petition. Your response can be as simple as stating that you admit or deny each numbered allegation in the petition. If the petition provides that "the parties were married in 1980", for example, your response to that allegation, if true, would be "admit."

If the petition provides, as most do, that the divorce is irretrievably broken, your response could be "admit" or "deny" depending on whether or not you agree.

If the petition contains an allegation that your spouse is disabled or unemployed and therefore, is in need of alimony, your response might be to admit that the party is disabled, but deny that the petitioner is in need of support.

An allegation that is admitted in an answer normally signifies that there will not be litigation as to that issue.

When you fail to respond

If you fail to file a response to the petition, then a clerk's default may be filed by the clerk that will allow, unless set aside by the court, the petitioner to proceed with an uncontested divorce without your objection.

Preparing an answer and counterpetition—the basics

The first page of an answer, like a Petition for Dissolution, sets forth the court name, the case number, and the style of the case.

Robert White, the fictitious Respondent in the preceding example, might respond in his "Answer" as shown below:

Answer to Petition for Dissolution

1. Admit for jurisdictional purposes.

2. Admit the parties were married, but deny they were married in 1982. (1983)

3. Deny that the marriage is irretrievably broken.

4. Admit that the parties have two children and admit that the parties should have shared parental responsibility, but deny that it is in the best interest that the wife be granted primary residential responsibility.

Counterpetition

A counterpetition is the respondent's petition for divorce. Like the petition, it contains separate allegations and requests for relief. A counterpetition is generally incorporated and follows the Respondent's answer.

Why you must file a counterpetition

The court cannot be your advocate. It does not have the authority or ability to grant you relief unless you request it. Therefore, if you file only an answer, but do not file a counterpetition (a pleading that sets forth what you are seeking from the divorce after a petition has been filed by the other spouse), then the court may not be able to grant your request. For example, if you want the marital home or alimony, make a specific request to keep the house and receive alimony.

Hot tip! If you cannot figure out how to file an answer or retain an attorney within the time allowed under your statute, file a response with the case number on it within the time allowed and ask that the court grant you additional time to file an answer.

Caution! When there are issues with the service (for example, you received the information in the mail, not by personal service or you have never lived with your spouse in the state your spouse has filed for divorce) it may be in your best interest to talk with an attorney about your options before you proceed.

Do you know where and how to serve the petition?

In order for the court to make a decision about your case, it must have personal jurisdiction (or authority) over both parties. To acquire personal jurisdiction, you must serve your spouse with the petition for divorce and allow them time to respond. A person is generally served with a petition by the deputy sheriff or a private process server.

In addition to providing copies of the filed petition, summons, and attachments, make sure to provide information to the process servers about where your spouse is living, who they are living with, their employment, their physical description, and the make and model of their car. The process server or deputy sheriff will file an affidavit with the court acknowledging when and how they were able to serve the petition.

Caution!

If a party has never lived in a state and was not living in a state during the marriage, the court may not have personal jurisdiction over that person. Personal jurisdiction is based upon the presence of a party in the state or minimum contacts with the person or ownership of property in the state. If you are the Petitioner and you have moved out of the state and now wish to serve your spouse and proceed in the state of your new residence, there may be jurisdictional issues that will prevent the court from ruling if it needs your spouse to submit to that court's jurisdiction. Consult an attorney for more information.

Hot tip!

If you are attempting an amicable divorce, do not serve your spouse at his place of employment or in front of the children. If possible, ask your spouse to sign an Acceptance of Service—a form indicating that they have received the petition, the summons, and exhibits thereto.

Are you in the right venue?

A venue is a geographical location or the county in which the court is located that a divorce may be heard. This is typically dictated by statute and based upon where there is the most information about the marriage. Although there are exceptions, usually, it is where the respondent lives or where the parties last resided as husband and wife.

Caution!

If you live in one county and your spouse lives in another, you may need to file in the county where your spouse lives to avoid a transfer of the action and a delay of the case. If you want to file in a county where you have moved after the separation, obtaining the agreement of your spouse to file in that county may avoid a costly delay and motions to transfer your divorce to another county.

Frequently Asked Questions:

Can my spouse file a petition for divorce without my signature?

Yes, a petition for divorce does not need to be signed by both parties unless it is a joint petition for divorce.

Can my spouse receive a divorce without me knowing it?

It happens, but only rarely. The petitioner is required to try to obtain personal service, which means delivery of the petition to you. However, if the Petitioner does not have your address, they may attempt an alternative service referred to in some states as constructive service. With constructive service, the petitioner attempts to obtain your last known address by contacting several sources. If your spouse is unable to find your address, the court may create an exception from having you personally served. In states allowing constructive service, the petitioning spouse must advertise in a newspaper in the area where the parties last lived together as husband and wife. After a certain number of notices have been published, the spouse may proceed as if the respondent was personally served.

What if my spouse doesn't agree that the marriage is irretrievably broken? Will the judge still grant my divorce?

Yes. Usually, only one person needs to request a divorce. A judge may recommend counseling but is not able to stop the divorce unless the other spouse is incompetent or some other jurisdictional prerequisite has not been met, such as service.

What if we try to reconcile after the petition is filed? Will the process continue anyway?

If you and your spouse agree to stop the proceedings in order to attempt reconciliation, then you or your attorney may ask the court to stop the court case temporarily. A Motion to Abate typically asks the court to stop the proceedings for a period of time between ninety days and six months. If reconciliation is successful, you may file a Notice of the dismissal.

If I forget to ask for child support or alimony in the petition, can I still get support?

The court may allow you to modify the petition anytime before the answer is filed or, if an answer has been filed, you may ask the court to modify your petition to include whatever requests or allegations you omitted.

What if I ignore the petition and don't file an answer?

If you fail to file an answer, the court, upon a request by the spouse seeking a divorce, may enter a default. If a default is filed, the spouse may proceed with an uncontested divorce and immediately seek a final hearing and final judgment.

If, for some reason, the answer is overlooked and not timely filed, do I have a chance to still file an answer?

Yes. As soon as it is brought to your attention, file the answer. If a default has been filed, immediately file a motion to set aside the default.

Do I have to sign the Petition?

A petition must be signed by you or your attorney. If you have an attorney, make sure nothing is filed without your prior review. Be aware that you are typically signing under penalty of perjury, meaning everything within the petition and any other affidavit including a financial affidavit or the UCCJEA affidavit is true to the best of your knowledge.

Can my spouse and I agree that neither party has to pay child support?

You may agree that neither party has to pay child support; however, in some states, such an agreement may not be enforceable and the court may inquire, prior to approving it, as to the reasons for such agreement. The court has the power to approve or disapprove it. Child support is owed to a child and not to the custodial parent.

What if my spouse is in the military and overseas? Can I still seek a divorce?

Yes. However, under the Uniform Military Soldiers Act, the spouse serving in the military may not have to answer until he is back in the states.

What if I don't believe in divorce and I don't want to answer the petition?

Simply not believing in divorce will not change the ways the divorce statute applies to you. You may seek a delay if you need time to go to marriage counseling, want to reconcile, or if you have a medical or mental condition that prevents you from proceeding.

What if I want to go to marriage counseling?

If your spouse will not agree to counsel, you may seek an order of the court by filing a motion to request marriage counseling. However, these requests are usually not granted unless both parties are willing to go to counseling.

What happens if my spouse dies before a final judgment is entered?

A death terminates the action, and it is as if the petition for divorce was never filed.

What if we signed a prenuptial? Do I still need to file a petition for divorce?

Yes. Unless provided otherwise in the agreement or by statute, you will still need to file a petition for divorce and serve it. If your spouse agrees that the prenuptial is binding and enforceable, you may proceed as set forth under the prenuptial. If not, then your spouse will be able to contest it by filing a motion to set it aside.

My spouse is stalling the divorce. What can I do?

You may file a notice of trial once the answer is filed. Alternatively, you may ask the court to set a case management hearing or another hearing and ask the court for their assistance in moving your case forward and resolving any outstanding issues. Finally, you may set a date for mediation.

Coming up...

Now that you have at least an understanding of the building blocks of a divorce—the petition, the answer and the counterpetition, it is time to avoid the dark hole of divorce—the muddled middle. Little happens there except time and money passes without much effort and after awhile, the process you hoped would be over in a few days, has now dragged on for more than a couple months. In the next chapter, we discuss the hazards of the muddled middle and how to hold onto your money that otherwise may be sucked out of you by attorneys or the court itself.

CHAPTER 8

AVOIDING THE DARK HOLE

If there is one area that seems to drag out forever it is what I call the muddled middle.

The muddled middle is like peering into a dark barrel and seeing only black. If you have an attorney, you may be waiting for documents from your spouse or for a hearing or mediation to take place. Unless you (or your attorney) plan this part of the process in advance, your divorce may stall and you may lose months – if not years— waiting for something to happen.

In a contested divorce, the middle of the divorce will likely be the most costly in terms of time and even money.

The Disclosure Dilemma

Prior to seeking child support, alimony, or a distribution of your assets by court order or even agreement, your state statute may require that you disclose multiple financial documents. Because of the voluminous amount of documents included on the list, judges rarely require strict compliance unless an attorney insists. To document compliance, attorneys draft certificates of compliance which provide in detail the items that they have and have not been produced. The list and the litigation used to enforce compliance create immense opportunities for repetitive contempt and enforcement proceedings and attorney fees. Under some statutes, each party, regardless of whether such documents have been already produced by the other party, must provide the same documents ordered under the statutory compliance. Common sense is not always common practice— especially in family law matters, but this is to at least theoretically assure that spouses are not hiding assets from the other.

Hot Tip!

From my experience, judges generally detest motion hearings to compel and to enforce compliance with the statutory compliance list. The same goes for enforcing compliance with other discovery requests such as interrogatories, requests to produce, and notices of depositions. Many judges see the hearings as the parties (or their attorneys) way to stall the case, increase fees, and waste time.

Why is your spouse refusing to cooperate?

A party's failure to provide the documents is not necessarily due to their desire to hide financial information. Although a spouse's failure to cooperate could flag a possible undisclosed asset, it could also mean their attorney (if they are not pro se) has not taken the time to ask or inform them about the disclosure request (or they are not aware of the rules), or the attorney did not have time to review the documents before the due date. Obviously, it could also be an attempt to delay the process for some financial or emotional leverage.

Can you receive attorney fees if your spouse doesn't cooperate?

Under some state family law rules and statutes, if a court has to order a party to produce the documents, they will also be ordered to pay the reasonable attorney fees accrued in bringing the motion and attending the hearing. Although this might appear sufficient to compel compliance, it often in the finally tally it generates nothing more than additional attorney fees for the requesting party. Just getting the issue in front of a judge creates opportunities for attorney fees to run amuck.

Time and effort to ask for attorney fees

In order to receive reasonable attorney fees for an opposing counsel's failure to comply, the requesting attorney must follow specific steps in an attempt to work out a solution without the court's assistance. First, they must call the opposing counsel to confer about their noncompliance. If the attorneys cannot agree, or the delinquent attorney avoids the calls or promises to comply but does not, often the attorney must follow up with a written request for the documents. If that fails, they must file a motion with the court, documenting their attempt to resolve the issue outside of court. Generally, if the disclosure is not forthcoming, then the attorney must obtain a hearing date for their motion to be heard. Because of the limited hearing time and an opposing counsel's schedule that allows little time to promote a competing agenda, coordinating hearing time could mean up to a three or six month delay. If time is available, the attorney seeking fees must draft an affidavit of their attorney fees and costs to justify the fee request.

Contempt/ Enforcement hearings – the scheduling headaches

A hearing on the disclosure, like most other hearings, may take as much as six months. Despite the hearing being scheduled and docketed, it may fail to take place because of the sudden unavailability of the attorney or judge. If a hearing begins as noticed, judges will often use whatever influence they have before a hearing begins to get the parties to agree so an order is unnecessary. In that case, documents are promised but because there is only an oral ruling and no order regarding attorney fees and sanctions for continued noncompliance, the opportunity to recoup attorney fees, at least at that stage, is lost.

Even if you are fortunate enough for the judge to rule and grant attorney fees, judges may delay the ruling regarding an amount of attorney fees or payment of attorney fees until trial. Sometimes this is because they do not want to delve into what an amount of reasonable attorney fees should be or because the attorney asking for attorney fees has failed to prepare or share the affidavit of attorney fees and costs with the court or opposing counsel.

Does a hearing guarantee compliance?

The party who is ordered to produce the discovery, despite the ruling, may attempt to delay the issue further by questioning what the order really means, and requiring another hearing to construe the order, or basically interpreting the ruling as narrowly as possible to avoid another motion for contempt or to compel. If the party refuses to comply within the time frame ordered or agreed upon, then the requesting attorney must repeat the process again.

The party who went to court to compel the disclosure cannot recoup the lost time or money. Even more frustrating, is that because of the skyrocketing attorney fees and delay of the divorce, the parties settle without ever seeing the requested disclosure. Attorney fees accrued in forcing compliance is usually reduced to a bargaining chip that is often swallowed up by bigger issues at mediation or in the party's settlement.

Hot tips to save more time and money!

1. **Before you file, gather financial documents.** Collect and copy bank statements, life insurance policies, deeds, bills, pay records, and income tax returns that prove the income, assets,

and debts acquired during your marriage. Return them as soon as possible so that your spouse may have their own copies. Take your copies to a safe place outside of the home. If you have retained an attorney, ask in the initial meeting for a copy of the disclosure documents that they will need from you or your spouse.

2. **Case management hearings.** Case management hearings, more than any other hearing may be the most helpful and least costly to you. Smart judges use them to eliminate otherwise long and laborious hearings from their docket and to shorten the length of time for resolution of issues, such as child support, the appointment of a guardian ad litem, or social investigator. The judge may also order a financial affidavit filed, child support or alimony payments to begin, or a mediation be scheduled. Case management hearings are generally set by the judge after your case has progressed to a certain point.

Family law judges who are sensitive to the needs of the litigants will have case management hearings to keep their docket moving. If the judge does not automatically set case management hearings, request one and ask the judge to establish deadlines for disclosure of documents or other types of discovery.

In addition, case management hearings allow the court to see you in a non-adversarial forum, and creates an opportunity for the judge to become familiar with your case

3. **Set up mediation time as soon as possible to ferret out the real legal or logistical issues even if it is only a disclosure issue that threatens to delay the divorce.** Generally, mediations set up to deal with the delay of discovery may give the parties an opportunity to resolve the

entire divorce before engaging in costly delays and attorney fees.

4. **Seek the assistance of other professionals.** If the contested issue is time sharing, you and your spouse may want to seek the assistance of a parenting coordinator or licensed mental health counselor with experience in working out time sharing and parenting plans. You may seek the expertise of an accountant or tax professional, who can guide you as to tax ramifications of paying and receiving alimony, the sale of real property and child support deductions.(These experts are generally included as part of a collaborative team. See Chapter on Mediation and Collaborative divorce.)

5. **Collaborate with your spouse regarding discovery documents.** If it is a high conflict divorce, meaning you and your spouse cannot agree on the color of the sky, you should continually reevaluate and prioritize how your time and money are being spent to compel discovery. Look for ways to subpeona the bank or record keeper of the entity producing the document as opposed to obtaining the documents through your spouse.

6. **Aim for moving through this phase within three months.** Sometimes, it takes longer than three months to schedule a temporary hearing. Scheduling a mediation may take only two weeks.

7. **Use only the discovery tools, such as interrogatories, depositions, and requests to produce necessary to gather the evidence to prove your case.** Although there are standard forms provided to gather documents (such as interrogatories, requests to produce and depositions) chances are you don't need to use them all. If your spouse cooperates with the statutory disclosure (if your state provides for this);

reevaluate what if any additional discovery is necessary. Do not assume just because other forms of discovery exist, that you have to use all of them. Tailor your requests to solicit only new and necessary information not previously received.

Coming up ...

For many, one of the most terrifying parts of the divorce process is preparing for and attending a hearing to request temporary relief. If you live separate and apart from your spouse, relief may come in many forms—child support and alimony, payment of household expenses, and temporary contact with your children. In the next chapter, we will examine the steps to take to receive temporary relief.

NOTES

CHAPTER 9

STEPS FOR RECEIVING
TEMPORARY RELIEF

If you need temporary child support, alimony, or exclusive possession of the home, but you and your spouse cannot agree and you have already attempted mediation, you will need to wait for the trial or file a motion for temporary relief.

How to set a temporary hearing

You (or your counsel) must draft, file, and send a motion for temporary relief with the notice of the temporary hearing to your spouse or their attorney.

What is a motion?

A motion is simply a request in writing that asks the court for temporary or permanent relief and may be titled simply "Motion for Temporary Relief". Other more common temporary motions filed would include Motion to Modify Visitation or Contact, Motion for Temporary Alimony, Motion for Exclusive Possession of the Marital Home and Motion for Child Support. Requests for temporary relief may also be included in the petition or counterpetition.

Preparing a motion for temporary relief – the basics

Like a petition or counterpetition, the first page of a motion for temporary relief will include the style of the case, the court in which the motion will be heard and the case number. The allegations establish the parties, the situation that is creating the need for temporary relief and the relief requested. Below is an example of a language and allegations frequently seen within a motion for temporary relief.

Motion for Temporary Relief

John White files this Motion for Temporary Relief and says as follows:

1. The parties separated on May 1, 2016. Since that time, the Wife has refused to allow the Husband weekend time sharing with the children or access to the children's medical and school records.

2. The children have missed one hundred days of school and are in danger of repeating the year.

3. The children's absences are unexcused.

4. The Husband believes it is in the best interests of the minor children that he have a primary residential responsibility *(or whatever the terminology used in your area)* of the minor children.

5. The Husband is in need of child support for the minor children and the Wife is able to pay for child support.

6. The Husband is in need of reasonable attorney's fees and the Wife is able to pay the same.

7. Wherefore the Husband requests that the court find and order that it is the best interests of the minor children that the Husband have primary residential responsibility of the minor

children, order child support be paid to the Husband, and order that the Wife pay reasonable attorney's fees.

The motion must be signed and include the same party contact information as the petition and answer.

Hot tips!

1. Filing a motion does not by itself secure hearing time. You or your attorney must also call and secure a hearing time with the judge's or general magistrates assistant, file a notice of hearing and send copies of the motion and notice to your spouse or opposing counsel. Failing to file and serve the motion and notice of hearing will likely result in the cancellation of your hearing.

2. Often there are family law rules requiring disclosure from the party seeking relief and limiting hearings until such disclosure has been made or there has been a waiver or stipulation by the other party.

3. To avoid delays, ask for temporary relief early. These hearings may take up to six months to schedule so secure a date as soon as possible after you have filed your petition. Filing a motion within the first thirty days after service of the petition may avoid the need of an emergency motion and hearing. In fact, if you have separated from your spouse prior to the filing the petition, include a request for temporary relief (temporary child support, alimony, exclusive possession of the home) in your petition for dissolution.

4. Some courts require that you attend a mediation on temporary issues before scheduling a hearing time so schedule a mediation on the temporary issues as soon as possible.

5. The court will only hear issues that have been raised in your

petition for divorce (or counterpetition) or motion for temporary relief. Your motion must include all the temporary issues you want the judge to decide. For example, if your motion only asks that the court establish time sharing, you cannot ask the court to award you alimony or to address an issue with the sale of the home. If you fail to include the issues in the motion for temporary relief and notice of hearing, your spouse or counsel will not have notice of the issues you want to discuss and therefore, may argue that they are prejudiced. If the judge agrees, the issues will not be addressed.

6. Visit and observe (if possible) another temporary relief hearing, preferably in front of the same judge or general magistrate. Typically these hearings are open, but you may call or email the judge's judicial assistant to find a hearing you can observe.

7. Verify that the motions, notices, and other documents you filed are within the court file.

8. Determine and gather the financial documents the court needs to rule on the temporary issues. For example, if there is a child support issue, the court will need information about your income and that of your spouse, the health insurance paid, childcare paid and by whom, and any special children's expenses

9. Make three or four copies of any documents you need at the hearing, including financial affidavits. This will allow a copy for the opposing party or counsel, the judge, the clerk and for you.

10. Before the hearing begins, determine the procedures, if any, to file an exhibit with the court.

11. Arrive early at the courthouse and look for a bailiff or judges' docket to verify that your hearing is still scheduled with the judge or general magistrate.

12. Do not bring babies or small children unless there is a childcare center within the courthouse.

13. Dress as professionally as possible. A coat for men is nice, but not required.

14. Do not interrupt the judge or be rude.

15. Do not interrupt the opposing party or counsel.

16. Do not speak directly to the judge or opposing counsel during the hearing unless specifically directed to do so by the court.

17. Do not write the judge a letter before or after the hearing. The judge is ethically prohibited from reviewing information that has not been shared with opposing counsel or your spouse.

18. During the hearing, direct all your comments to the judge, not to opposing counsel.

To prepare like an attorney—do this.

To prepare like an attorney, you need to determine the law that governs the issue, understand the facts that affect the court's decision, and offer the court the backup documentation (the exhibits), prepare your testimony, witness questions, and points that support your request for the relief you are seeking.

For example, if your temporary hearing is with regard to child support, familiarize yourself with the state statute regarding how child support is calculated and what information the court needs to do the calculation. In most states, this would include providing your pay stubs, your spouse's pay stubs (or income tax return if their pay stubs are unavailable), your childcare receipts, health insurance payment records and your financial affidavit. You may also need to bring information (perhaps your calendar or journal) to determine the number of nights that the children spend with you versus your spouse. Make sure that your documents reinforce your testimony and have copies of exhibits necessary to share with the court.

When to use general magistrates

Most courts have general magistrates who preside over temporary relief hearings or final hearings. Although they are not judges, they assist in handling the family law docket and have limited authority to hear certain types of cases.

Using a general magistrate over a judge offers several benefits. First, they are often quite experienced and may know the area of law better than the judge assigned to your case. You may be able to get a hearing scheduled with a general magistrate before that of a judge. If you have an attorney, ask about their experience using the general magistrate.

Caution! Although temporary hearings are generally scheduled for thirty minutes or an hour, if both parties want motions heard and there is inadequate time on the docket, then the "temporary" hearings may be continued time and time again. A temporary hearing like this can generate an enormous amount of attorney's fees and costs, and result in more delay in reaching the trial stage. They, like hearings on discovery motions, use up the monies reserved for the trial and often leave the parties hanging on for months, if not years, with only a temporary order, but not a final judgment. Consequently, if one side is more financially set than the other, this creates a disparity between the parties and the one who is without monies to continue the litigation, is often forced to settle.

When to file for an emergency or expedited hearing

File an emergency pleading if there is a physical or emotional threat to you or your children. Similarly, if there is a risk that an asset will be depleted prior to its distribution or if you cannot live on your own without financial assistance, call the judicial assistant or case manager for the judge and ask to schedule an expedited or emergency hearing. Failure to take advantage of emergency or expedited hearing time could delay a ruling for months and threaten the loss of your home or create a risk of harm to your children. If you are pro se, this is a time to reconsider that decision and retain an attorney.

Some judges define an emergency as only when a person's life is at stake and rarely grant time for emergency relief hearings. Others calendar time for both emergency and expedited hearing time. Occasionally, the court will publish a court's docket online for your review.

Hot Tip! Be careful not to title every motion as "Emergency" or "Expedited". Limit yourself to one emergency or expedited hearing, and only if it is truly an emergency. Labeling every motion as expedited or emergency may only result in angering the judge and your motions being ignored.

Frequently Asked Questions:

If I obtain primary residential responsibility or custody of my child at the temporary hearing, will that order become permanent at trial?

Although temporary orders are typically titled "temporary," often they become the basis for final orders. It is in your best interest to ask the court to insert specific language in the temporary order that it may be modified and is not binding on the permanent order.

Is a temporary order modifiable?

Yes, it may be, but that is assuming either that you both agree to the modification or that you are able to obtain another hearing time and show that the circumstances have changed.

Is a temporary order appealable?

In many states, a temporary divorce ruling is not generally appealable. It is also not subject to a motion for rehearing.

Can I go to a temporary hearing without filing a financial affidavit?

You can go to a temporary hearing without filing a financial affidavit; however, if you are requesting relief, your failure to provide a financial affidavit and comply with the financial disclosure may prevent you from receiving relief. Similarly, if you are the payor spouse, your failure to file the appropriate disclosure could result in the court relying on the evidence by your spouse as to your income.

My husband refuses to provide financial disclosure prior to the hearing. Will I be able to get relief?

Judges are all different and may have certain practices that require you to continue the hearing unless there is another way to provide the necessary evidence. That is why it is important to gather all information about pay for both you and your spouse before the petition is filed and to leave it with a trusted friend until you need it.

Coming up ...

Why mediation is the best way to resolve your case without spending your children's college money and having a nervous breakdown.

CHAPTER 10

HOW TO USE MEDIATION OR THE COLLABORATIVE TEAM APPROACH TO FINISH YOUR DIVORCE

Perhaps the worst part of divorce is watching parties who were once committed to spending the rest of their life together, now turn and spend all their energies and resources on destroying each other. In a spouse's emotional need to beat, punish or annihilate the spouse, they end up draining their assets and leaving irreversible emotional scars on their children. Despite our society's resort to family courts when our marriages or other relationships fall apart, the legal system often does more harm than good. Families walk away with emotional, financial, and relationship scars that follow them the rest of their lives. Our family courts have become battlegrounds—not hospitals— for wounded families.

A tale of two mornings. Court or mediation—you choose.

Let's look at two scenarios—one in which a person begins a trial and the other in which a person attends mediation. As you read the scenarios, think about which of the two would you prefer.

Trial scenario: After circling the parking lot for thirty minutes, you have finally found a parking space. You forgot that you might need to pay for parking, but you find three quarters and sink them into the parking meter, knowing you will probably have a parking ticket when you return. It is already 8:15 and your attorney told you to show up by 8 a.m. to go over your testimony. You lock the car and halfway into the courthouse your turn around to retrieve that file you were suppose to take with you. You retrieve it. It is now 8:20. Your trial starts at 8:30. You stand in a line that wraps all the way around the inside of the courthouse lobby. It's the security and metal detector line. After the deputies inspect everything in your briefcase and purse, another twenty minutes have passed. It's a delay you didn't expect. You now have visions of being held in contempt for being late to your trial. You're perspiring and remember you didn't use deodorant. You stand in another line to ask where your courtroom is because your attorney is no longer in the place he said he would be. You take the elevator and eventually find the courtroom and wait outside on a bench for someone to come and tell you to come in. A grim bailiff with guns directs you inside the courtroom. Your attorney is arguing with opposing counsel about the admissibility of evidence, what the judge will or won't allow, and last minute settlement options. Your ex isn't budging.

A judge walks in and you stand. You notice the judge isn't the one you were expecting, the one you liked and knew your case the best. That one had a medical appointment. This one is a substitute. This one has already made their mind up you're not getting what you want because you were twenty minutes late and you have already set them behind for the entire day. You remember substitute teachers from school. You never liked them very much. The tension is high as the judge asks if you and your attorney are ready to begin. The court reporter is in place, the boxes of exhibits are rolled in and the judge swears in the parties. It is the culmination of six months, a year or two years of work. Now everything rests on the next three to six hours or sometimes the next few days.

During the opening statement, your attorney forgets to mention your request for attorney's fees. You whisper to the attorney, but are told to "write it down." You write down – "you forgot to tell the judge I need repayment of attorney fees." Your hands are shaking.

The judge nods and says, "Call for your first witness." For a moment you wonder where the witness stand is and then the grim bailiff points it out. He tells your spouse to get rid of his gum. You swallow yours.

You have already forgotten everything that you were supposed to say and not say. During the direct examination, you realize your attorney hasn't made enough copies of all the exhibits so opposing counsel has to use yours during cross-examination. He stands over you and literally breathes down your neck. Both he and the judge notice that you round off all your expenses to "00". You told your attorney to change that after you read *Divorce Made Simple*. Your attorney forgot.

The judge tells your attorney he doesn't care what you think about your husband's new girlfriend and the affect it might have on your elementary school age daughters. After two or three hours, the judge calls your attorney to the bench and your attorney comes back to you and whispers, "I think we should settle. It's not going well." You taste everything you ate for breakfast.

Let's compare that with the level of tension and stress at a mediation.

Mediation scenario: You pull up to a parking space outside a two story building in the suburbs, walk into a small office and are greeted by a receptionist. After being offered a cup of coffee and some snacks, you speak with your attorney alone (if you bring one). Your attorney reminds you of what you told them about needing to walk away with so much for alimony. You eventually are called into a different room and sit down across from your significant other and next to the mediator. After introductions, the mediator asks you to tell them why you are there and what you want to discuss and resolve during the mediation. You talk about the issues with the mediator in a way organized by the mediator.

Breaks are taken often and you speak with the mediator, alone, or with your attorney. You want to talk to your spouse alone about why it's important that the kids have Christmas morning with you and you speak together without your attorneys and he agrees. After a few hours, you and your spouse agree to many issues, but not on the alimony amount. You worry that there could be an impasse and you both might up in front of a judge at some point in the future. Although it has been only three months since the petition was filed, you worry that if you don't settle today, the divorce could drag on for months.

There is a saying that the worst day of mediation is better than the best day in court. Neither solution is perfect. However, in mediation, there is breathing room for resolution of issues depending on the needs and personalities of the parties. It is not a one size fits all approach. Although there is tension, you may compare the stress induced from participating in a trial versus that from going to mediation as the stress induced from watching a high techno thriller as compared to watching a family drama.

Mediation—the benefits, process and path.

Mediation and other non-adversarial approaches to conflict resolution allow both parties an opportunity to state their needs on a level playing field. The parties may speak about the issues in a way that is comfortable for them without rules that govern what they say and when they say it. In trial, the court's options as to how to resolve issues are limited according to legal precedent and statute. In contrast, there are endless ways parties can agree in mediation. Once a mediation is concluded, even if the parties are unable to reach total agreement, the experience usually does not leave the parties with so much disdain and anger that they are unable to ever communicate again. Unfortunately, one of the consequences of going to trial is the elimination of all trust and communication between the parties.

The level of tension starts with the announcement of a divorce and escalates until there is a final judgment signed by the judge. Stress hormones and cortisol are continually released in the blood stream, which if the parties are already physically challenged, can create additional emotional, mental, and physical challenges.

Benefits of mediation.

1. You may attend mediation at any time voluntarily upon you or your spouse's suggestion. A court may also order you to attend mediation.

2. Mediation allows you to have input and control over the outcome of legal issues.

3. Mediation can be done with or without attorneys and through court paid or private mediators.

4. The cost of attending mediation is much less than paying an attorney to litigate in court. You may pay a mediator per hour much the same way you pay an attorney. Just like attorneys, the price varies. Often the court will offer mediators at a lesser rate to reduce court dockets. The cost of a private mediator is generally higher than court mediators. Whatever the cost, unless there is an agreement or order otherwise, the fees are split between the parties and are less expensive than paying an attorney to appear in court.

5. Mediation is confidential and less costly than a trial.

6. If the parties are able to reach an agreement in mediation, it shortens and simplifies the divorce process. If parties have successfully avoided the divorce war and escalating anger, they may be able to resolve their issues and have lunch on the same day. The parties still have money left in their pocket to go out for lunch. In total contrast, after a trial, many of the parties have tapped into their savings, retirement, and kids college funds and are hoping they have enough money to pay their next month's rent. Mediation and collaborative processes also save time. With mediation a divorce can be completed within three months; a trial can extend a divorce to more than three years.

How to prepare for mediation

The best way to prepare for mediation is to know your case and to make sure your attorney, if you have one, knows what you are seeking from the divorce. Have a wishlist of what you are seeking, a list of issues that you're willing to negotiate to a lesser outcome, and a list of issues that you are willing to have a judge decide.

If you have complex and highly contested issues, such as child support, alimony, and parental contact, your best decision may be to find an experienced attorney who knows how to negotiate and reach an agreement that you will not look at in a week and wonder what you were thinking when you signed it.

How to choose a mediator

Choosing a mediator. Mediators are generally lawyers, however, that is not always the case. They may also be mental health counselors, psychologists, financial advisors and certified public accountants. The best choice for most divorce mediations is a mediator that has family law experience. Even if parties are unrepresented, mediators can assist parties by preparing a settlement agreement, or a draft of the agreement reached during mediation. That settlement or mediation agreement may be attached as an Exhibit or Addendum to the Final Judgment. Although just like attorneys, you may choose a mediator who is certified, do not exclude attorneys who do not advertise as "certified mediators." In the nineties and beyond when the courts began suggesting mediation, thousands of attorneys became certified. Through the years, however, mediators had to weigh the cost of keeping up that certification, which was generally a 40 hours course for each area of law – for example – family mediation, civil, mediation and so forth. Many of those who became certified early on allowed their mediation to lapse as found that it did not make much of a difference to their clients if they were certified. Just like hiring an attorney, don't get caught up with credentials. Look for an attorney with family law experience.

Assure a mediator's neutrality. Mediators are neutral third parties and, like judges must disclose any interest in the outcome and as well as any conflict of interest. Sometimes there is a gray line as to what constitutes a conflict of interest. Obviously, if the mediator has previously served as an attorney for a party, that is a conflict of interest. But there may be other conflicts that the mediator should, but do not always disclose.

Who to bring with you for advice

Often parties are tempted, even when they have attorneys to bring family members or friends with them. This is not usually a good idea. Although the moral support is a good idea, having their phone number may work better. The presence of individuals who are not affected by the outcome of the divorce may do nothing more than increase the anxiety level for your spouse who may resist agreement if they think the idea are being promoted by someone other than you.

Similarly, do not bring your children, even if they are teenagers, to a mediation, unless there is a specific agreement by all parties including the mediator to do so. Often parties will bring children to mediation to influence the other parent regarding alimony, child support, and contact issues.

Bring an attorney. Mediation is definitely an event that you want to bring as much legal knowledge and wisdom with you as possible. Attorneys with family law experience who understand the legal ramifications of your agreement's terminology and the can answer you're "what if" scenarios that may happen after the final judgment could save you time and money you might otherwise lose because of an oversight at mediation.

The Process

What to expect in mediation

Introduction. To begin a mediation, after short introductions, mediators may share their experience and expertise before giving the parties a roadmap as to what will happen in the time set aside for their mediation. Rather than having a judge, who listens and acts as a gatekeeper for all evidence that a party presents and then rules on the evidence that he or she has allowed, a mediator encourages communication in a non-adversarial way. The mediator is a person that is neutral and does not have an interest in how the parties decide an issue.

Opening statement. Mediators will ask each party or their attorney, to outline the matters that the parties want to resolve. The issues may be resolution of temporary matters, discovery issues such as production or location of certain documents, or issues such as timesharing of children, alimony, or child support and equitable distribution that would otherwise require a trial. The mediator begins with the easiest issue, so parties understand that they are capable of resolving issues.

Caucus. Mediators may separate parties immediately or during the negotiation of issues. The mediators meeting with one party and their attorney is called a caucus. Sometimes the mediator will leave the parties separated until the most difficult or all of the issues are resolved. Even if parties have met separately with a mediator during the mediation, the mediator brings the parties together again before the mediation is concluded to review what if any progress they have made and how to proceed regardless if they have been successful or unsuccessful.

Preparation of a Mediation agreement. Once most of the issues are resolved, the mediator will call for both parties to meet together to sign a mediation agreement. Sometimes it is just an outline that attorneys will agree to flush out later in a Settlement Agreement that will contain the formal language that they need to preserve the integrity enforceability of the agreement. Other times, the mediator will provide a more thorough agreement that the parties may attach to a Final Judgment and file with the court.

A settlement or mediation agreement's length will vary depending on the number and complexity of the issues.

What's the difference between a mediation agreement and a settlement agreement?

Divorce settlement agreements may be called by different names (post marital, mediation, collaborative) but they basically are intended to resolve the issues that are set forth in the petition for dissolution. The names typically reflect the means (collaborative, mediation) or the time in a relationship (premarital, postmarital) by or in which they were produced.

Usually, agreements, unless produced under fraud or duress, stop the madness of the divorce and allow the parties to get back to grieving, healing and resuming their lives. Drafting and executing such an agreement, however, should not be a task attempted without an understanding of the terms and conditions in the agreement. A thorough review of the agreement must be made before signing to avoid unintended consequences.

Before signing, look for these issues.

The process of obtaining an agreement, whether by mediation or settlement discussions, can be long and laborious. When parties are close to resolution, they are also often tired and "over it." However, it is at this time, when most mistakes or omissions happen. In fact, some, if not all attorneys use a strategy of making mediation a long and laborious event for the sole purpose of wearing the other side down so that they are tired and ready to give up and go home.

Before signing your settlement or mediation agreement, make sure you have read it at least three times and understand what it says and then answer these questions.

1. Is the language vague?

2. Are there provisions within the agreement that do not indicate when a certain action is going to take place?

3. Does it list out the options the other party has if the action does not take place in the time frame or manner set forth in the agreement?

4. Are there blanks? If you do not have legal counsel, make sure that the actions required by the agreement have been performed or time frames for the action agreed to in their agreement are plainly set forth.

5. Is there a time when your spouse is moving out of the house?

6.   Will they deed you the house?

7.   Have you discussed a holiday schedule with your spouse?

8.   A summer time schedule?

9.   Who is going to drop off and pick up the children?

10. Who will watch the children if they get sick?

11. Who can babysit?

12. When does alimony end? When does it start?

13. Is there life insurance to secure the alimony?

14. How will you tell if the spouse responsible for keeping life insurance actually honors the agreement?

15. What happens if you have two children and one child turns 18, how is child support going to end or be modified?

16. If there is a retirement account or pension, does it require an order from the court to release the monies? If it requires an attorney to draft the proposed order, called a Qualified Domestic Relations Order (QDRO), who will pay for the attorney to draft it? When will be drafted? How much is going to go to each spouse?

17. Is there a child support order that will be drafted? Will monies be automatically deducted from your spouse's paycheck?

Should you draft your own?

You can draft an agreement that reflects the issues that you have resolved regardless if they are temporary or permanent resolutions. However, unless you have very few issues to resolve (for example who is going to get the dog, the car, pay the last month's rent) drafting your own agreement could potentially lead to a dangerous scenario.

Differences in education, financial, or legal knowledge or experience, may give you or your spouse an advantage in the drafting or review of the agreement.

If you or your spouse are still dealing with the emotional chaos created by the divorce, thinking through the consequences of certain provisions may be difficult, if not impossible. A human tendency is to rush through signing agreements to stop the emotional pain regardless of the cost. This, however, could lead to post judgment issues and spending twice as much to correct, modify or clarify a mistake or omission in the original agreement. If a person is unprepared for a divorce, to receive the news that the spouse wants a divorce at the same time that spouse presents them with a settlement agreement, leaves the spouse in shock woefully unable to think rationally because of the trauma. This is often how spouses who are worried about their risk of paying alimony or losing significant pension benefits that "their wife did nothing to contribute" will "win" in a divorce. The danger in giving a document to an unsuspecting spouse under these conditions, is both parties usually end up in court arguing over a Motion to Set Aside the Settlement Agreement because of fraud, duress, or overreaching. This potentially adds a year or two delay in receiving a final judgment and an attorney fee bill in the tens of thousands.

How you can protect yourself from a sloppy agreement

To avoid big mistakes, take a draft of the agreement to a family law attorney and ask him to review and give you his opinion as to enforceability and completeness of the agreement. This is money well spent, especially if you are presented with a settlement agreement by your spouse at the same time you are told of his need for a divorce. Spending the money for an attorney to review this agreement may provide you information as to what you are legally entitled to and may save you thousands of dollars and years of ongoing post-judgment conflict. Specifically, ask the attorney about the effect of the agreement under certain "what if" scenarios. Spending time with an experienced family law attorney (not your friend who practices patent law in another state) to help you to draft or review the agreement before its execution is money well spent.

What to do if your mediation fails

If your case stalls after mediation or fails in mediation, make sure you or your attorney file a Notice of Trial. While the filing of the notice itself does not put you on a path to resolving the matter within three or even six months, it may be enough to move the rudder closer.

Often cases will settle after a touch of reality is forced upon parties, either through the filing of notice of trial or by the judge in a pretrial hearing. Although judges do not like to predict how they will rule, as this usually means they have prejudged the case, an attorney will often inquire of the judge in front of the client just so that they can hear a warning from the judge himself about the waste of time and money incurred in a trial. Divorces settle on the courthouse steps before the trial starts, after opening statements and even midway through the trials.

The next step after reaching an agreement.

Often the agreement provides that the following mediation, one or either party may proceed to the final hearing without the other being present or without further notice to the other side.

Caution! If all issues have not been decided, do not proceed to a final hearing until all issues have been thoroughly flushed out in the agreement. Often there is an agreement for one party to do something, but the agreement fails to specify the timing or date for such action. If you have an attorney, this is something that they should double check before the final judgment is prepared, so that the need for an enforcement action after entry of the final judgment is eliminated.

Hot Tip to Salvage Mediation.

To salvage a mediation, make two lists—your best day and your worst day in court. Now pick your battles that really matter in order to drive home an agreement that you can live with without it costing you your entire savings for attorney fees for your attorney or the fees for your spouse's attorney.

Caution! Your failure to attend mediation after being ordered to do so may result in the court ordering you to pay the other side's attorney's fees and costs associated with your failure to comply with the court order. In addition, you may be held in contempt by the court for willfully refusing to abide by a court order.

What if you change your mind? There are very few ways to modify or quash an agreement that has been signed at mediation. Modifying or quashing agreements signed in mediation is very difficult because the court assumes you knew all the information you needed before you signed the agreement. Generally, once you and your attorney sign a mediation agreement, it is enforceable unless it was procured under fraud or duress.

How does a collaborative divorce differ from mediation?

Team Approach. A collaborative divorce, like mediation, is non-adversarial. However, rather than the parties focusing their energies on what is best for themselves, it is a team approach that encourages spouses to focus on the family unit instead of themselves individually.

Cost. Unless lower cost collaborative divorce is offered for those with less income, the process tends to be more expensive than mediation. In addition to the party's attorney, it often requires the presence of a mental health expert and a financial expert. It remains however generally less expensive than going to trial.

Use of the same expert. If the parties have complex issues, such as valuation of a business, or complex children issues, the process could potentially save the parties tens of thousands of dollars by eliminating a trial and the need for dueling experts. Experts in a collaborative setting, however, technically, work for the family unit and not the party or attorney who hires them.

Confidentiality. Like mediation, another advantage of the collaborative model is that the process is confidential. Papers regarding a party's financial wealth, and even the settlement agreement, normally available for the public view, are not filed in the court system.

Final hearing to conclude divorce. Like a mediation, once an agreement is reached in the collaborative setting, either party is usually free to go to a short hearing with the judge to obtain a divorce.

Caution! A drawback of the collaborative divorce is that if the collaborative approach fails, each party must retain different attorneys prior to filing a petition for dissolution or litigating in court.

Four-way conferences

For parties and their attorneys who know how to communicate and have remained amicable, four-way conferences are the quickest and least adversarial of any of the other methods of resolution. Usually, parties are ordered to meet (and their attorneys) only before filing a pretrial stipulation. This is after much of the damage has been done to the parties and the children and frankly, is used after the parties have already spent all their liquid assets on attorney fees. At that point, attorneys and experts realize there is not enough money in the bank accounts for trial costs and fees.

Hot tip! If you are represented by counsel, ask them to set up a four-way conference in the first thirty days after a petition has been filed.

Frequently Asked Questions:

If I sign the agreement at mediation, do I still have to go to court?

The court may allow you to file an executed marital settlement agreement or mediation agreement with a stipulated Final Judgment that has been approved by both parties and their attorneys as a way to eliminate a final hearing. Alternatively, a judge may require one party to attend an exparte hearing to assure that the mediation agreement has been signed freely, voluntarily and without duress and that certain statutory requirements have been met such as residency and that all issues have been addressed to the satisfaction of the court or individual judge. Call the judge's office that your case has been assigned to and ask. Alternatively, refer to the judge's local administrative rules.

What if we can't agree in mediation?

If you can't agree, then you may sign an agreement outlining the issues you've agreed to and reserving on the issues you can't decide until a trial is set and a judge can decide those issues. If there is a complete impasse, the parties should file a Notice of Trial in your matter. Settlements often happen prior to the trial when parties are faced with giving the issues to a judge to decide for them.

Wisdom: Be cautious, although agreement is showing forward movement, often one issue impacts the other. If possible, try to resolve the entire agreement at the time of the mediation or continue it.

What if I live out of state? Do I have to travel to attend mediation?

Often courts and state rules allow parties to attend mediation by phone. It may be necessary, however, to file a written request to attend mediation by phone.

What if I change my mind?

Although parties sometimes change their minds, unless both parties are willing to amend the agreement to reflect the change, then it will be necessary for the party with the change of heart to file pleadings with the court asking that the agreement or parts of the agreement be set aside. The reasons may vary depending on the circumstance and the laws of the state. For instance, you may suggest that you were under duress, under the influence of medication or alcohol, or that you relied on information that your spouse gave you which was false or misleading.

Coming up…

So you have an agreement that is without blanks, appears to have the right legal terms (you reviewed the Principles section of this book before you signed it) and have reviewed it with an attorney. Now what? A final hearing will seal the deal. Find out what you need to do to prepare in the next chapter.

CHAPTER 11

YOUR FINAL HEARING

Don't confuse a final hearing and trial. Your final hearing is generally a summary hearing that is two or three minutes long—just long enough for the court to assure that formalities have been met. Assuming all issues have been resolved in mediation, judges routinely sign the final judgment—the order ending your marriage—at the final hearing.

Preparing your Final Judgment—the Basics

The court will expect that one of the parties will provide the draft of final judgment that they want the judge to sign prior to or at the time of the final hearing. If you are pro se, you will submit a final judgment with the language that you are requesting. It is important that this proposed order has been reviewed by your spouse or their counsel before you submit it for signing.

If this is an uncontested divorce, coming to an agreement about the language and terms in a proposed final judgment may be a nonissue, especially if there has been a mediation and you are simply attaching the agreement to the Final Judgment and asking the court to approve it. (Compare this, however, to a trial scenario where a judge may take as much as six months or longer to return a final judgment after the trial, even if you and your spouse submit proposed final judgments.)

You may find forms for final judgments at your state supreme court's website (Appendix attached) or at the law library.

A Final Judgment of Dissolution of Marriage like a Petition for Dissolution of Marriage includes the court in which the action takes place, the case number and the style of the case on the first page. The Final Judgment includes findings that the court will make at the time of the final hearing about the marriage and the settlement agreement as well as an order dissolving the marriage.

FINAL JUDGMENT OF DISSOLUTION

The court, having heard testimony of the parties on August 12, 2016, makes the following findings:

a. Marriage. The parties were married in Orlando, Florida on August 1, 1995.

b. Residence. Both parties have been residents of Orlando, Florida for more than six months before the commencement of this action.

c. The marriage of the parties is irretrievably broken.

d. The following children were born of the marriage. John, born August 1, 1996, and Susan, born August 1, 1997.

e. Shared parental responsibility. It is in the best interests of the minor children that both parties share parental responsibility.

f. Stipulation: The parties have entered into a Mediation agreement dated December 24, 2016.

g. The court finds that the Mediation agreement was entered into freely, voluntarily and without duress.

h. Wherefore the court it is adjudged that;

1. The marriage is dissolved.

2. The Wife's name is restored to Betty Black.

3. The settlement agreement is accepted and ratified.

4. The court reserves jurisdiction to modify and enforce the final judgment.

Signed by: The best judge on this __ day of December 2016

What to bring with you to a final hearing

Make sure to bring identification such as a driver's license with a photo ID to the final hearing. If your driver's license was issued prior to the filing of the petition for dissolution, it will help prove your residency. If you are not represented by counsel, bring a proposed final judgment and a copy of the Mediation or Settlement agreement if the original has been filed in the court file. Expect the judge to ask you to identify the signatures on the end of the agreement and to inquire if the agreement was signed voluntarily and without duress.

How to change your name

If you want your name restored to your maiden name or another name, the easiest way to do so is at the time of the final hearing instead of a separate action after the divorce. Request in your petition for dissolution that you want your maiden name be restored. Then, make sure it is included within the final judgment and that the spelling of your restored or new name is correct. If the request for your name change was overlooked, ask the judge before your hearing begins, to grant your name change. Be prepared for the court to ask if you have ever been found guilty of a felony, filed bankruptcy, or are asking that your name is changed for any ulterior purpose such as defrauding creditors. You will also need to bring a photo identification to the hearing.

Once the final judgment is signed, you may want to get certified copies from the clerk's office to make necessary changes in your social security and driver's licenses and passport identification.

Caution! If only your spouse attended the final hearing, don't wait any more than five days to follow up and obtain your own copy of the executed Final Judgment from the lawyer's office or from the clerk's office. If there has been a clerical mistake, you want to make sure that this is corrected immediately. Often after a final hearing, a lawyer may put away the file and forget to send out copies of the final judgment.

Coming up...

The purpose of the next section is to familiarize you with certain legal principles and concepts, terminology surrounding common divorce issues. It is not an outline for every divorce issue. Recognize that although most states follow the same principles for divorce issues, each state has its own decisions and statutes.

Shared parental responsibility, joint residential responsibility and primary and sole residential responsibility sound the same. Should you be concerned with nuances? The next chapter will shed some light on these terms.

THE PRINCIPLES

UNDERSTANDING THE LEGAL
ISSUES IN YOUR DIVORCE

CHAPTER 12

CONTACT WITH YOUR KIDS

If you have minor children and anticipate litigation about contact or with whom your children should live with, familiarize yourself with the legal terms, criteria, and resources that courts use to render opinions in this area.

Judges and attorneys rely on numerous mental health professionals to provide information to them about your relationship with your children and your parenting skills. If you are facing litigation in this area, you must understand the roles these experts play.

Sole parental responsibility versus shared parental responsibility

Shared parenting, or shared parental responsibility, as it is sometimes called, allows both parties access to their children's medical and educational records regardless of where the child lives or who the child lives with. The principle contemplates that the parties have the desire and ability to make decisions that are in their child's best interest. In most instances, parties share parental responsibility and the concept anticipates joint input and decision making.

Sole parental responsibility is the opposite of shared parental responsibility and allows one parent to make all decisions with regard to the child unilaterally. Failing to understand the difference between sole and shared parental responsibility and signing an agreement giving the other parent "sole parental responsibility" jeopardizes a parent's rights to unfettered contact and access and the right to have input into parental decision making.

The mix up between the terms shared and sole parental responsibility often happens when pro se litigants draft an agreement themselves or pull a form from the internet. At other times, it is when an attorney drafts a parenting or settlement agreement and asks an unrepresented spouse to sign it and the spouse does so based upon the promise of the other parent that they will never interfere with the contact.

As a judge in final hearings, when I reviewed signed settlement agreements, I would inquire from the parties what they believed the term sole parental responsibility meant and if there was some reason why shared parental responsibility would be detrimental to the child. The parties would often be surprised by my question. I couldn't tell if they were surprised that I was actually reading the final judgment (instead of just signing it blindly) or that I was asking them what they thought it meant. Inevitably, at least one would be relieved that I caught the mistake before I signed their order.

In Florida, for a court to approve sole parental responsibility, the court must make a finding why shared parental responsibility is detrimental. Often pro se litigants do not understand this condition and present the final judgment without it. Judges who sign but do not read orders could potentially miss the term leading to litigation post judgment.

Time sharing

After the court makes a determination that shared parental responsibility is appropriate, the judge must then decide time sharing. Without an agreement, time sharing can be the judge's most difficult decision. Because of the litigation and hostility that was created over the term "primary residential parent" and the confusion with that term and shared parental responsibility, some courts no longer refer to time spent with the child as visitation, but as residential time sharing and contact.

Several states now require that the court start with the premise that parents have equal time sharing. However, the terms "primary residential responsibility" and even "custody" may still be referred to in conjunction with or separately from time considerations. For instance, the parties may be granted equal time with the child, but one parent may still be labeled primary residential parent and given more day to day responsibility. Unfortunately, despite the changes in legal terminology, time sharing is still one of the most litigated issues. The parent who has greater contact also may receive support or perks to assist in the stability and support of the child including but not limited to greater child support.

Best interest test—to decide time sharing

If you are unable to settle issues of time sharing and parental responsibility, you must become aware of the factors the court uses to determine the best interests of the child. Although parents don't usually review the court's criteria until they are faced with a custody battle, it should be reviewed even prior to filing for divorce. Negative interactions with your child or your spouse during the litigation can impact the court's finding that you are the spouse best suited for having majority of time with and responsibility for the children. Although the best interest test may differ from state to state, it is the overriding guideline that all courts use.

The court has a responsibility to assure that the child's relationship with both parents is not only maintained but where possible, strengthened during and after a divorce. How well the one parent reinforces and strengthens and encourages the relationship with the other parent may become the most important criteria. Other factors that the court must consider is the ability of one parent to provide for the basic needs of the child, if one parent has historically been the primary caretaker and if one parent is more involved in the child's extracurricular activities and school.

Often parents will change their work schedule right before a trial as a way to obtain more time sharing or the primary residential designation. For example, if one parent has traveled extensively for the last five years and has little contact with the child because of their employment, that person may quit or change jobs just prior to the trial to show the court that now they are available to have equal time or primary residential responsibility of the child. Waiting to the last minute to make an employment change may not be a smart tactical move as the court may question your motive and credibility.

Caution! Securing a court reporter is always necessary to protect against judicial errors and safeguarding your rights as a parent. Although a family judge has immense discretion in the decision making, do not waive your ability to appeal the judge's order by failing to bring a court reporter.

Hot Tip! If you are asked why you are seeking primary residential responsibility or why you want the child to live with you, simply answering that "you love your child" does not differentiate you from the other parent as the court usually assumes that both parents love their children. Stating that you love the child, you have always been their mother or father, the child has said they want to live with you, or that the other parent is too busy or too self-centered are reasons the court may discount. The court assumes that both parents love their children. The issue is how are you better suited to take responsibility for your child or children? If you criticize the other parent, be prepared to give examples and not make general statements degrading your spouse.

Do not wait until the day or evening before a court hearing or trial to review and document how these statutory factors or similar ones, favor or handicap the court's finding that it is in the best interest of the minor child that you have more overnights and greater contact with your children. Reflect and genuinely consider your parenting strengths and weaknesses as well as to those of your spouse before you are on the witness stand.

Enrolling in a parenting class about assisting a child in a divorce is an excellent way to learn about the factors the court uses to determine best interests. State statutes or court orders often require that the class be finished before trial or entry of a final judgment. The class is an excellent way to learn what behaviors affect the child's ability to process the divorce.

How will a temporary order or stipulation affect the final outcome?

Sometimes a judge or general magistrate will award primary residential responsibility and carve out timesharing at a temporary hearing, even when there is little time for testimony. Of more concern to a parent who feels short changed at a temporary hearing is that a decision rendered at a temporary hearing is often used either directly or indirectly to support a final decision at trial regarding residential responsibility or contact. If you are in this situation, it is important to keep a log and calendar during the pendency of the divorce with specific dates and relevant events. Your calendar should document your actions and those of the other parent which may either support or detract from the best interest criteria and the judge's initial decision at the temporary hearing.

When is rotating contact appropriate?

In ordering timesharing, the court may consider alternatives to the every other weekend schedules ordered by the courts in the past.

Rotating time sharing such as week to week or a rotation of certain days is frequently ordered. For example, week to week rotation contemplates the child staying one week with one parent and then the next week with the other. The week may start on any day. If week to week is not ordered, the court may order a 2/4 split or 3/4 split so that the child spends three days a week with one parent and four days a week with the other parent in some repeating pattern. Obviously, the age and needs of the child should weigh heavily on any time arrangement. If the child is in preschool, then this rotating week to week schedule may be a viable alternative. However, if the child is in grade school, middle school, or even high school, a rotating schedule may not work as well because of the child's specific need to keep all their stuff in one place or the need to keep transitions at a minimum.

Similarly, if there is a conflict between the parents, the court may want to limit the number of transitions so as to restrict the child's exposure to the parental conflict. The court may also avoid parental conflict by having the child picked up at school or daycare.

What is a Parenting Plan?

Many states now require that the parties draft a parenting plan when they have minor children. A parenting plan is a document created to govern the relationship between the parties relating to decisions regarding the children's education, health care, physical, social and emotional well-being as well as parental contact and communication. It must contain a time-sharing schedule for the parents and the child. The parenting plan must be approved by the court, and if the parents can't agree, the court may choose between the ones submitted to the court. Alternatively, the court may draft its own.

Besides you, who may offer their opinion about time sharing?

To prepare for trial, the court on its own, or by recommendation by one of the attorneys, may appoint a psychologist, a mental health professional, a guardian ad litem, or social investigator to assist the court with the determination of the time sharing.

Psychologist. This is an expert that may render a professional written opinion to the court usually based primarily on psychological testing, as to which parent should be granted primary residential responsibility, which parent should have greater time with the child or which parent should be given exclusive decision making responsibility. To make this determination, the psychologist will often seek an evaluation of both parents and children.

Social investigator. A social investigator may be a counselor or someone trained in conducted social investigations. In some jurisdictions, a social investigator is a paid professional who routinely conducts social investigations as a neutral third party for the benefit of the court.

Mental health counselors Courts may order or the parties themselves may retain mental health counselors to assist in the divorce process. Typically mental health counselors are ordered if the parties have minor children and are in high conflict or have a history of domestic violence. The courts may also order an attachment evaluation, which is similar to a social investigation and a guardian ad litem report. An attachment evaluation is generally less intrusive than a full psychological evaluation but provides the court with information about the parties and the child's relationship with the parents from the observations of extended family members, teachers, and the children themselves.

Guardian ad litem. A guardian ad litem is a person chosen to represent the child. In some jurisdictions, this person actually becomes a party to the divorce. As a party, the guardian ad litem attends hearings, mediations and unless settled prior to the trial, will testify as to their findings and observations during the trial. The court will appoint a guardian ad litem if there are allegations of child abuse or that one of the parents has an addiction or mental illness that potentially threatens the security, safety or wellbeing of the child. Although they may cost less than a psychologist or mental health counselor unless they serve in a pro bono role, they usually require a retainer and charge hourly. It is important to understand and be willing and able to pay the guardian's charges prior to a court ordering a person to serve as a guardian. The guardian typically provides a written report regarding their observations and recommendations about the children's interaction with each parent at each parents home, conversations with the child, and with other significant people in the child's life, including, but not limited to grandparents, neighbors, and teachers.

Parenting coordinator. Another person that a court may utilize in a divorce proceeding with a minor child is a parenting coordinator. A parenting coordinator is generally appointed in high conflict cases to eliminate the courts need to micromanage the parties during the divorce process. However, unless the parties specifically agree or there is a court order otherwise, the parenting coordinator does not have the ability to make major decisions regarding residential responsibility or time sharing.

What is the UCCJEA?
Uniform Child Custody Jurisdiction and Enforcement Act (UCCJEA)

The UCCJEA is a uniform law regarding the determination of jurisdiction for custody matters. All states except Massachusetts has adopted the Act. The Act gives the court exclusive jurisdiction (authority to make decisions regarding a child's parental contact and residency) to the courts in the child's home state, which is where the child has lived with the parent for the last six consecutive months prior to the commencement of the proceedings. If the child has not lived in the state for at least six months, then a court must determine if the state has significant connections with the child or if another state would be better suited to hear the matter.

The Act also has an emergency provision so that if the child is in danger and needs immediate protection, the state which otherwise would not have jurisdiction may enter a temporary emergency order.

Coming up...

Besides the tug of war about how the children should be shared, the court often is asked to divide up the marital property. In the next chapter find out if there is a method that a judge uses to divide up the assets or if it's totally arbitrary.

NOTES

CHAPTER 13

HOW DOES A COURT DIVIDE YOUR STUFF?

Couples often exert too much energy arguing to the mediator or the judge about how and why they should receive the stuff they have accumulated during the marriage. When and if this happens, they may be consumed with the idea they have to have an asset because it is "sentimental", they earned it and the other spouse didn't help at all, or they need it as a trophy from the marriage. To avoid this unnecessary flexing of muscles, and the exorbitant time and attorney fees generated by it, it might be helpful to understand how and why judges ultimately make the decisions they do about the division of property. Here is the long and short of it.

Equitable distribution versus Community property states

In all but nine states, courts use what is referred to as "equitable distribution" to figure out how to divide your property. The property subject to equitable distribution may include your home, other real estate, intangible property like stocks and bank accounts, and personal property such as cars, the grill, and big screen television.

If you live in a state that follows the equitable distribution method, the court order dividing your property may be based in part, on factors that the court has been given by statute to determine what is fair and equitable. The equitable distribution method, like a determination of best interests, gives judges discretion in how much weight to give the factors and therefore in the ultimate decision. Judges in states that follow the equitable distribution method, start with the goal of dividing the assets is to equitably, which does not necessarily mean fifty-fifty.

To illustrate the analysis used by courts, consider the following scenario. During the time of the marriage, the wife earned a half million dollars because of a break through patent she developed. The Wife deposited the money in a joint bank account. Should the husband be entitled to one half of the monies in the bank account? If you are in a state that recognizes equitable distribution factors, that answer may depend on particular situation and how the court and what statutory factors the court uses.

In states using the equitable distribution method, the court uses factors such as the age of the parties, the duration of the marriage, the sacrifices of either spouse to support the other, the earning capacity of the other spouse and others. So in this scenario, what if the parties had been married for twenty years and the husband had given up career opportunities to support the wife's endeavor to develop this patent? Do you think the court would take that into consideration? What if the had only been married for two years and the husband himself had patents worth millions of dollars? Would that change things? Probably would.

In contrast, the nine states that call themselves community property states- California, Arizona, Louisiana, New Mexico, Texas, Washington and Wisconsin, Idaho and Texas, split the value of the asset or debt down the middle and do not consider factors. It doesn't matter how the assets are titled or if they are accidently placed into a joint bank account. They are divided equally.

An example of how a court might divide your stuff – the rationale

To illustrate, how a court might attempt to equitable divide property, let's assume that the parties own a home valued at $250,000 with a mortgage of $200,000. They have $35,000 in a savings account. They also have two cars, one that is paid for and the other with an existing lien that the parties pay every month and personal property valued at $5,000. The Wife just received an inheritance from her mother's estate for fifteen thousand dollars. The Husband has a 1966 Mustang convertible that his father gave him before the marriage valued at the same amount. How would the court divide the property?

Guidelines

In this example, it is helpful to recognize that there are a few guidelines, in addition to the statutory factors that a court uses to decide what property a spouse will receive in the final judgment.

First, assets that belonged to the party before the marriage are considered premarital, and absent extenuating circumstances, they are not regarded as marital assets. So the Mustang would remain with the Husband.

Second, assets like an inheritance, that a spouse receives during the marriage, absent circumstances, will also be set apart from the marital properties that will be included within equitable distribution. The Wife, therefore, would not have to share her mother's inheritance.

Finally, if an asset is not free and clear of debt, the debt is usually transferred with the asset. Whoever wants the new car will probably also have to shoulder the monthly payment.

Given these basic guidelines and assuming that the judge is not likely in this scenario to waiver from an equal division of the property, let's look at how the assets listed above might be divided.

First, if the wife indicates she wants the house, the court would put the equity in the home (not the fair market value but the value minus the debt) in her column.

Assets:	Value
Marital home	$50,000
Savings account	$35,000
IRA	$6, 500
Value of Car with debt	$2,000
Value of car that is paid off:	$10,000
The total value of the marital property is	$103,500

To render a division that is equitable, the court, if it decides to order that the home be transferred to the Wife, would order that she continue to make the payments on it. To achieve an equitable distribution, it might order that the savings account and IRA be the property of the Husband. If the Wife wanted the new car, she would also be ordered to pay the car payment. The Husband would be given exclusive title to the remaining car that is paid off and valued at $2,000. Under this scenario, each party would walk away with roughly $51,000.

Wife	Husband
$50,000	$35,000
$2,000	$6,500
	$10,000
$52,000	$51,500.

The court would ask the parties to make a list of the personal that each wants and would jump up and down and perhaps send them back to mediation before it took the time to sort out the pots and pans. Technically it could might award $500 more of the personal property to Husband to equal the columns, but few courts will worry about being that exact when deciding personal property.

How to save time and money.

Dividing up assets should be an issue that is determined and agreed upon in mediation. Unless there are circumstances that you believe would influence the judge to use the statutory factors to order an unequal distribution, equitable distribution should be a rather simple division problem.

To prepare for mediation, parties should identify and prepare a list of marital, nonmarital and premarital property. A good place to start your list is to refer to the assets and debts listed on your financial affidavit. Then for each asset, attach the value of the asset from a third party source if available. For example, if you had a marital home, attach an appraisal or a comparative market analysis prepared by a real estate agent. You would also attach the latest statement from the mortgage company indicating what is left on the mortgage.

Then each of you should prepare a list of the personal property you want to retain from the marriage. Usually this resembles the following— Wife wants the dining room furniture, Husband wants the guest bedroom furniture. Wife wants the china, Husband wants the art carvings and big screen television. If you are able to communicate with your spouse about how to divide the personal property (the pots and pans, etc.) you will save time and money at mediation or trial.

Caution: In most cases, it doesn't make sense to pay attorneys to argue about assets, especially personal property. Consider the hourly fee of an attorney, multiply by ten and ask how many televisions or barbecue grills you could purchase with this money. You could probably buy yourself several. Similarly, unless there are investments and issues that complicate a straight division of marital properties, it seldom makes sense to go to trial over the single issue of equitable distribution.

Coming up...

If one spouse is unemployed, does that mean the other will automatically be ordered to pay alimony? In the next chapter, we'll discuss the factors courts consider when awarding alimony and the types of alimony that a court may award.

CHAPTER 14

ALIMONY

HOW A COURT DECIDES ALIMONY

Alimony is a payment by one spouse to another for their support. In the last twenty-five years, there has been a trend away from alimony awards. Part of the reason for this may be because most women are employed outside of the home in some capacity. Although alimony was historically awarded to women, because of the changes in social and employment norms, men may also request and qualify for alimony.

Guidelines

The court uses statutory guidelines when considering alimony awards. For example, before the court awards alimony, it must find there is a need by the requesting spouse for such support and that the payor spouse has a reasonable ability to pay. The court's analysis stops if either of those questions are answered with a "no".

However, if the court finds there is a need and there is a corresponding ability to pay, it may then consider factors such as the duration of the marriage, the financial circumstances of the parties, their physical and emotional health, their age, their marital and nonmarital assets, their income and earning abilities, and their contributions to the marriage. Specific factors vary according to state.

The court also must determine the distribution of the marital assets before there is an alimony order. The reason is clear. If one party receives $500,000 from a bank account, they may not have a need for alimony. Alternatively, the court may award alimony to offset inequities caused by a division of marital assets.

There are several types of alimony including permanent, rehabilitative, durational, bridge the gap, lump sum, and temporary.

Permanent alimony

Permanent alimony is monthly support paid to a spouse in an amount that the court or the parties believe will ensure the maintenance of a spouse during their lifetime or until the alimony is terminated pursuant to the terms of the party's settlement agreement or the final judgment. Generally, permanent alimony terminates upon the death of either spouse or the remarriage of the requesting spouse.

If the court finds that there is a need for support for some period of time, but not until the death or remarriage of the receiving spouse, the court may consider ordering other forms of alimony.

Durational alimony

Durational alimony is generally awarded when permanent alimony is inappropriate (such as the marriage was of short duration). In most cases, the duration of this alimony will not exceed the length of the marriage.

Rehabilitative alimony

Rehabilitative alimony is awarded to assist a party to become self supporting through training, education, or the development of new skills. It generally includes basic support for the time necessary to receive the training or education as well as the payment of the training or educational costs. For example, a spouse who requested rehabilitative alimony to attend a culinary school for two years could receive monies for basic living expenses for two years plus the cost of the culinary school. The alimony may be paid either periodically or in lump sum.

Bridge the gap alimony

*Bridge the gap alimony i*s awarded when the spouse has a level of education, work experience, or skill but needs a short period of time (generally up to 2 years) to become self-supporting and to allow a party to make a transition from being married to being single.

Lump sum alimony

Lump sum alimony is payment of a fixed and definite sum and is in the nature of a final settlement between the parties. It may be awarded not only as a monetary sum but also in the form of real or personal property. Often a court will call an award of one spouse's interest in a home to the other spouse lump sum alimony.

Temporary alimony

Temporary alimony is the payment of support for some period during the pendency of the divorce.

Coming up...

In the next chapter, we'll discuss how most states calculate child support.

NOTES

CHAPTER 15

HOW DOES THE COURT
DECIDE CHILD SUPPORT?

Child support is a court-ordered payment to assist with payment for the needs of the party's child or children and is usually based on the parties' income.

The Formula- Three Models

Child support is determined by a formula. There are three basic calculation models used throughout the United States. Most states use the model based on the concept that the child should receive the same proportion of parental income that they would have received if the parents lived together in an intact household. To determine the amount of support, the income of both parents is pooled and spent for the benefit of all household members.

In Florida and other states, the basic child support obligation is usually determined by using child support guidelines. The schedules are dependent upon the parents combined gross income and the number of children in the family. The final child support calculation may take certain financial factors into consideration including income deductions for social security, federal and state income taxes, health insurance paid for the parents and children and the number of overnight contacts parents have with the child or children.

When determining child support, a trial court is required to make findings of fact regarding the income. Such findings include the gross and net earnings of each party.

Courts in nine other states use a percentage of income model which is based on a percentage of the noncustodial parent's income. Three states, Delaware, Hawaii, and Montana, use the Melson formula which starts with the assumption that support of others is impossible until a person's own basic support needs are met.

Does the court consider child care and health insurance in child support?

All guidelines incorporate a "self-support" amount for the payor and consider the health care expenses of the children, by insurance or other means. Special additions to the formula are available in most states to incorporate child care expenses and varying amounts of contact between the noncustodial parent and the children as well as deductions for support of children unrelated to the marriage, and subsequent children born to the payor.

Child support awards follow equitable distribution and alimony

Courts using the method that take into consideration the earnings of both parties are not able to calculate how much child support to order until decisions regarding equitable distribution and alimony have been decided. This applies to mediation agreements as well.

For example, if a spouse is ordered to pay $2,000 in alimony to the Wife, this is money that is not available to pay child support. Similarly, if the Wife is receiving $2,000 a month in alimony, she will have a greater income with which to provide for herself and her child and this will factor into the child support equation.

Pay to play

Often a spouse will withhold a child's contact with the other paying parent until child support is paid or brought current. In most states, however, child support and contact are separate and not tied to the other and it may be reversible error for the court to so rule.

When does child support stop?

Generally, child support lasts until the child turns 18, graduates from high school or becomes self-sufficient.

Unemployed spouses

If a spouse is unemployed, the court may impute income to pay child support if there is a determination that the parental has the ability to work and the unemployment or underemployment is voluntary.

Coming up...

Attorney fee awards are a mystery for both attorneys and their clients. The next chapter will shed some light on the subject.

NOTES

CHAPTER 16

ATTORNEY FEES

THE ISSUE THAT EVEN ATTORNEYS HATE TO DISCUSS

Of all the remaining issues, the one that gives the parties the most heartburn is fearing that they will be ordered to pay the other's attorney fees. If you are in need of attorney fees, you must request them in the petition, the counter petition, or in a motion. Parties may request attorney fees in the beginning of the divorce before any litigation or mediation, in the middle (when a spouse is no longer able to pay attorney fees), or before or after a trial.

If you want to obtain an attorney, but do not have the ability to pay attorney fees and have issues that will require lengthy or multiple hearings or mediations, schedule a hearing for attorney fees as soon as possible to avoid delays.

To avoid the delay and costs incurred in scheduling a hearing on a motion for attorney fees, parties and attorneys should attempt to stipulate to the payment of reasonable attorney fees. Stipulating as to the amount and payment method allows the divorce to continue and avoids the fees generated asking the court for, or defending against, an award of attorney fees.

The parties may also stipulate, if necessary, to liquidating a marital asset to pay for attorney fees. Emotions often escalate after parties are forced to sell an asset that has been painstakingly saved or accrued by the efforts of one or both of them. After becoming aware of the potential loss of personal or marital assets, they may decide to avoid court and resolve issues through mediation or a collaborative divorce. Alternatively, their anger may escalate and they may seek to retaliate against their spouse for the forfeiture of their property.

"You should be entitled to attorney fees" is not a guarantee

If an attorney tells you that "you should be entitled to attorney fees," do not assume this to mean you will be reimbursed for all your attorney fees and costs. There is no guarantee that you will ever collect on attorney fees even if there is an order to do so. Consequently, you may not have the ability to pay off the fees borrowed on a credit card or to repay the friend or relative who lent you the money with the promise you would "pay it back after the divorce."

When the bills go unpaid, attorneys have few choices

If you pay an initial retainer, but cannot pay the monthly bill after your retainer is gone, your attorney may consider the financial risk associated with representing you. There are few available options for attorneys who want to move a case along but are not paid. They may represent you without being paid (rarely), withdraw from your case even before a hearing on attorneys fees, stop action on your case until you find the monies to continue or the court orders that your spouse pay attorney fees and the monies are received. Some attorneys will agree to barter with a client who can provide services or an asset in exchange for continued representation. If possible, discuss these scenarios with your attorney before signing a retainer agreement.

The two questions that must be answered with a yes.

Typically, if there is a request for attorney fees, the court implements a two-part analysis. First, it must determine if the requesting spouse is entitled to the payment of reasonable attorney fees and if the other spouse has the ability to pay all or a portion of them. Second, the court must determine if the attorney fees charged were reasonable.

This analysis to determine if a party has the ability to pay the other spouse's attorney's fees follows that of an alimony support award to determine if there is a need for fees and if the other party has the ability to pay.

Often a vicious cycle is created when a spouse needs attorney fees, but are not able to prove the other spouse's financial ability because they refuse to disclose financial information. Their need to compel disclosure prior to obtaining attorney fees often creates attorney fees and months of delays. (See earlier chapter about Avoiding the Dark Hole and the Disclosure Dilemma). Unfortunately, it is this exact scenario that the spouse with the greater financial resources seeks to create to obtain a better bargaining position. Often referred to as an economic squeeze, a spouse with little or no money for attorney fees, at the brink of losing their attorney, is often forced to settle for less than they may deserve. In fact, before a divorce is finalized, many of those who began with attorneys end up pro se or unrepresented.

What the court looks for before ordering fees

If the court finds that one party is in need of attorney fees and the other party is able to pay them, the court will review the attorney's billing records to determine a reasonable award of attorney fees.

Determining what is reasonable requires the attorney for the requesting spouse to disclose the amount of fees and when and how the fees were incurred. If there is no stipulation between the parties as to a reasonable fee amount, the judge will review and determine if the time charged for tasks such as drafting pleadings, preparing and attending trial was reasonable. For example, would it take an attorney four hours to draft a simple petition for divorce? Sometimes the court will inquire whether the work could have been performed by someone else other than the attorney. For example, copying will not be a task that a party can be reimbursed for by the other spouse because it is secretarial and does not require an attorney's skill or training to complete. Travel time to and from the courthouse is also generally not reimbursable.

The courts may also inquire about the attorney's hourly fee and level of experience. Before the court awards a dollar amount as a fee award, it will make a finding that the hourly amount charged was reasonable for the level of experience and qualifications of the attorney and in keeping with the attorney fees charged by other attorneys in the community.

Finally, a judge may not order that all your attorney fees and costs be paid. If you request anticipated attorneys fees and costs, your attorney must provide an affidavit of anticipated fees and costs. The anticipated costs may include services, such as payment of a court reporter for the depositions of certain individuals, a vocational evaluation or the service of subpoenas to third parties. The court may grant the motion in part, awarding some, but not all of the monies necessary to pay these costs. Similarly, if your attorney asks for forty hours of attorneys fees to prepare for a trial, but the court believes only twenty hours is reasonably necessary, your attorney may weigh the chances of you being able to pay the difference later or limiting preparation to twenty hours. Alternatively you may offer the attorney security to prepare for trial as they believe is necessary.

After a trial there is often no award of attorneys fees

Judges often deny a motion for attorney fees when the marital assets have been equally divided and the parties are both self supporting regardless of other considerations such as the disparity of income. Typically this occurs when parties litigate custody issues and their attorney fees may well be more than fifty thousand for each of them. Litigants relying on an award of attorney fees, then find themselves stuck with an enormous attorney fee bill, with few choices other than paying off a credit card over time with higher interest rates, filing bankruptcy, or stiffing the attorney and hoping the attorney does not sue for payment of fees or collect purusant to a charging lien. Their decision to pursue a ruling regarding contact or primary residential responsibility, although more important than fighting over the barbecue grill, leaves both children and parents traumatized. Often it is the child's college education account that is emptied by the parent's need to pay attorney fees.

Coming up...

Finalizing your divorce is a time to grieve and celebrate. Find out why in the next chapter.

NOTES

CHAPTER 17

HOW WILL YOUR STORY END?

You have the ability to choose how this story ends. It has been an emotionally draining time, even under the best circumstances. You have determined the path and the process. You have worked with a counselor or an attorney or have struggled to do it by yourself and hopefully relied on a couple good friends to get you through. Now you have chosen to spend time and money to end it in court or have finished it with mediation. If you have been through the process and are not done, you still have decisions to make. You can end it and walk away or fight it out and try to get what you want regardless of the law, the judge or anything else. Hopefully, you will choose what is best for you and your children.

After you have a final judgment, you have another decision- to let it go or to hang on and let the anger and disappointment consume you. I hope you will decide to let it go.

This too will pass

The entry of your final judgment signals the end of a chapter in your life and the beginning of a new chapter

Celebrate the end of the process, but take time to grieve the end of your marriage. Divorce does not have to mean a time of war; it can actually be a time of letting go of the conflict that brought you to this stage and begin to heal and think of forming a new relationship with your spouse.

Give your children a gift they will thank you for.

I hope that eventually, you will be able to recall the good things of the past and work together with your former spouse to support the best part of your marriage- usually your children. If you have been able to work through issues with your spouse during the most emotional and difficult time in your life, then you probably will be able to continue to have a working relationship with your spouse.

Being able to communicate with your spouse without resurrecting those feelings of anger, disappointment or betrayal is a tribute to your emotional, mental and spiritual strength. Moreover, remaining strong under difficult circumstances may be one of the best gifts you can give to your children. I often reminded couples in my courtroom that their children loved both of them. To criticize your spouse in front of your children is like knocking them down, they are made up of both of you. Don't shame them because they want to continue a relationship with your spouse. They need that to understand who they are and to understand that the divorce is not their fault.

They will carry the memories of this divorce with them their entire life. Those memories will be either good or bad. They will be there to reassure them that difficult situations can be resolved without a war. Or the memories will be there to haunt them about the trauma they experienced as a child of two people who could not resolve their differences amicably.

Remember there will inevitably be events during your child's life that both you and your ex spouse will want to attend. Don't miss out on soccer games, high school, and college graduations, weddings, the births of grandchildren just because you haven't been able to move on. Being able to put your past aside and letting whatever good memories of your marriage remain and others fade away may be in your best interest as well as your children's.

You may recall seeing Prince William speak about how the death of his mother, Princess Diana, continued to plague him and his younger brother more than twenty years after the tragic event. The same could be true for your children about your divorce. Children will grieve the loss of their family as they knew it. Instead of leaving the remnants of a storm that will continue to haunt the dark places in their psyche, give your children a memory that will reassure them that like their parents, they can successfully navigate and make it through the rough weather in their life.

MORE RESOURCES
ABOUT DIVORCE

I hope this book helped in some way to simplify an often confusing and heart wrenching process. Consider joining DivorceMadeSimple, a support forum, on Facebook, to ask questions and share your divorce experiences with others who are walking down the same road.

Join our mailing list to receive information about webinars, online courses, updates and handouts at Divorcemadesimple.com.

Leave a Review

If you enjoyed this book, please consider leaving a review on Amazon. Thank you.

LEARN MORE AT

DIVORCEMADESIMPLE.COM

APPENDIX

Family Law Forms by State

AL- www.judicial.state.al.us

AK- www.state.ak.us/courts

AZ- www.superiorcourt.maricopa.gov/SuperiorCourt/
FamilyCourt/Index.asp

AR- http://courts.arkansas.gov/forms-and-publications

CA- www.courts.ca.gov/selfhelp.htm?genpubtab

CO- www.courts.state.co.us/Self_Help/Index.cfm

CT- www.jud.state.ct.us/webforms/default.aspx?load_catg=
Family#searchTable

DE- http://courts.state.de.us/family/divorce/forms.aspx

DC- http://www.dcbar.org/for-the-public/legal-
resources/pro-se-pleadings.cfm

FL – www.flcourts.org/resources-and-services/court-
improvement/problem-solving-courts/family-
courts/family-law-forms.stml

GA- www.georgiacourts.org/georgia-courts/court-forms

HI- www.courts.state.hi.us/self-help/divorce/forms

ID- https://courtselfhelp.idaho.gov/publications#Divorce-
Children

IL- http://www.law.siu.edu/selfhelp/

IN- http://in.gov/judiciary/2684.htm

IA- http://www.iowalegalaid.org/issues/self-help/familylaw-self-help-forms-and-instructions

KS- http://www.kscourts.org

KY- www.kyjustice.org/divorceforms

LA- http://www.familycourt.org/main/inside.php?page=
forms

ME- http://ptla.org/court-forms

MD- http://www.courts.state.md.us/family/forms/divorce.pdf

MA- http://www.mass.gov/courts/selfhelp/family/

MI- http://michiganlegalhelp.org/self-help-tools/family

MN- http://www.mncourts.gov/Help-Topics/Divorce.aspx

MS- http://www.mydivorceusa.com/divorce-forms/
mississippi-divorce-forms.htm

MO- http://www.courts.mo.gov/page.jsp?id=3832

MT- http://courts.mt.gov/library/topic/end_marriage

NE- https://supremecourt.nebraska.gov/forms

NV- http://www.familylawselfhelpcenter.org/forms/
divorce-forms

NH- http://www.courts.state.nh.us/fdpp/divorce_parenting.htm

NJ- http://www.judiciary.state.nj.us/prose/index.html#family

NM- https://supremecourt.nmcourts.gov

NY- http://www.nycourts.gov/forms/familycourt/index.shtml

NC-
http://www.nccourts.org/Courts/CRS/Policies/LocalRules/
Documents/1621.pdf

ND- http://www.ndcourts.gov/ndlshc/FamilyLaw/
FamilyLaw.aspx

OH- https://sites.google.com/a/clermontcountydomesticcourt.org

/checklists-and-forms/home

OK- https://sites.google.com/a/clermontcountydomesticcourt.org
/checklists-and-forms/home/divorce

OR- http://www.courts.oregon.gov/OJD/OSCA/JFCPD/Pages/
FLP/Divorce-Separation-Annulment.aspx

PA- http://www.pacourts.us/learn/representing-yourself/
divorce-proceedings

RI- https://www.courts.ri.gov/PublicResources/forms/Pages/
default.aspx#

SC- http://www.sccourts.org/forms/indexSRLdivorcepacket.cfm

SD- http://ujs.sd.gov/Forms/divorce.aspx

TN- http://www.tsc.state.tn.us/help-center/court-approved-
divorce-forms

TX- http://texaslawhelp.org/resource/commonly-used-fill-
in-forms-online

UT- https://www.utcourts.gov/ocap/index.html

VT- https://www.vermontjudiciary.org/family/divorce

VA- http://www.the-divorce-source.com/virginia-divorce-
forms.htm

WA- http://www.courts.wa.gov/forms/

WV- http://www.courtswv.gov/lower-courts/family-
forms/index-family-forms.html

WI- http://myforms.wicourts.gov/wizards/family/
getting_started/confidentiality_and_computer_access

WY- https://www.courts.state.wy.us/LegalHelp/Forms:

Family Law Residency Requirements by State

AL – 6 months

AK – 30 days, with
  children- 6 months

AZ – 90 days

AR – 60 days

CA – 6 months in state, 3
  months in county

CO – 90 days

CT – 12 months

DE – 6 months

DC – 6 months

FL – 6 months

GA – 6 months

HI – 6 months

ID – 6 weeks

IL – 90 days

IN – 6 months

IA – 12 months

KS – 60 days

KY – 60 days separation, 6
  months

LA – 12 months

ME – 6 months

MD – 12 months

MA – 12 months

MI – 180 days

MN – 180 days

MS – 6 months

MO – 90 days

MT – 90 days

NE – 12 months

NV – 6 weeks

NH – 12 months

NJ – 12 months

NM – 6 months

NY – 12 months

NC- 6 months, separation
  12 months

ND – 6 months

OH – 6 months

OK – 6 months

OR – 6 months

PA – 6 months

RI – 12 months

SC – 3 months if both
  parties are residents,
  12 months if only one
  party is a resident

SD – 90 days

TN – 6 months

TX – 6 months

UT – 90 days

VT – 6 months

VA – 6 months

WA – none

WV – 12 months

WI – 6 months

WY – 60 days

ANOTHER BOOK BY THE AUTHOR

An Illusion of Normal

In an era when speaking of mental illness was taboo, the author learns from an early age not to talk about her mother's bizarre behavior. Now her mother's escape from a would-be killer threatens to expose the family secret. They are not a normal family.

Finally, after her mother's extended stays in mental institutions, she accepts that her Mom will never be normal. That, she assumes, makes her abnormal as well. She wrestles against her father's abuse and constant shaming of her and her faith and wonders if she will ever feel normal in an abnormal family. Did God make a mistake? Why is she in a home where she doesn't feel loved or accepted? Is there a way for her to break away from the shame that holds her captive?

An Illusion of Normal is the riveting and award-winning memoir of a life of a child whose mother suffers from paranoid schizophrenia. At times shocking and heartbreaking, her story exposes the darkness in a home tormented by a parent's mental illness and the light that shows the way out. An inspirational story for anyone looking for hope in difficult circumstances.

An Illusion of Normal, the true story of a child's survival in a home tormented by mental illness, is available on Amazon Kindle and paperback. Click here - http://amzn.to/2qB48bk

Made in the USA
Lexington, KY
16 January 2018